Bernd C

The Secret of Karmic Relationships

7 Steps to Clear Up Your Relationships

Deep Life Counselling –
Finally understanding what is going on!

www.karmische-beziehung.de/karmic-relationship

Edition 05/2019
Title of the German first edition:
Das Geheimnis karmischer Beziehungen
www.karmische-beziehung.de
Original Edition 2013

Cover: © Fotolia | FreshPaint, O. Glushenkov 39133206
Cover design: Gabor Gerec, Michael Baumgartner,
Photo credit: © Fotolia | Jim Mills 11653311, Winne
68695960, Gcro Images 40150900, shock 63871500, Klikk
31714600, Ioannis Kounadeas 45990260 + 22252201,
Konstantinos Kokkinis 27981390, Klara Viskova 13176510,
A. Dudy 16198427 |

Publishing and printing: tredition GmbH,
Halenreie 40-44, 22359 Hamburg
978-3-7469-6604-5 (Paperback) | EN
978-3-7469-6605-2 (Hardcover) | EN
978-3-7469-6606-9 (e-Book) | EN

Other languages

Das Geheimnis karmischer Beziehungen | DE
ISBN 978-3-7469-4743-3 (Paperback)
ISBN 978-3-7469-4744-0 (Hardcover)

Тайна кармических отношений | RU
978-3-7469-6129-3 (Paperback)
978-3-7469-6130-9 (Hardcover)
978-3-7469-6131-6 (e-Book)

I do not know your personal life circumstances and I am therefore not aware of what kinds of experiences have shaped your life either. On the following pages I would like to consider the principal influences on possible experiences in terms of "relationships" and "karmic relationships" in particular. In the sense of this guide I see "karmic" as a cycle of cause and effect which again and again leads to seemingly unsolvable conflicts at relationship level. Cause and effect are often confused. More often than not, the real cause is neither known nor apparent.

Thoughts and insights are usually very fleeting. You would do well to equip yourself with pen and paper so that you can write down your aha-moments.

The guide includes many "fruits" for you. I would urge you not to "enjoy" them all at once. Please take your time to slowly absorb and process the information. Otherwise there is a risk that you might get over-whelmed without even noticing.

Tip:
Write down any incentives for action which come to you spontaneously while reading. That way you will easily create your personal check-list which you can then implement step by step.

Table of Contents

We only notice
the limits
we live in
when we
try to change them.

Preface

For many years, life had presented me with more questions than answers.

What you get to read below has been written because people like you and I and all those we love or would have wished to love, deserve an answer.

Especially when it comes to being lovesick, feelings are turned upside down, the soul is confused and the affected person often feels utterly desperate. Many people feel helpless and clueless with regards to relationship issues. In "karmic" relationships, life seems to go off the rails uncontrollably. In this guide you will find out why many consultants, seminars and therapists cannot help you. Above all, you will finally get a clear view of fundamental connections that have never been published before in this way. Practical ways to achieve change, heartfelt love and many aha-moments are also included here.

Even for me, life still holds many secrets. I would however like take this opportunity to share with you all the things I have found out so far. Before we set out on our journey to unravel the secrets, I would like to assure you right now: beyond the suffering there is still hope.

Anyone who follows this path accelerates the healing process for all of us. The topic "relationship" can basically only be understood if we are willing to consider the complex structures involved more precisely. I would like to give you the opportunity here to study a few of the key areas in more detail and hope that these basics can help you find targeted new ways to your personal freedom. More and more, you will be able to recognise, understand and change what perhaps still forms the mysterious framework of your sleepless nights.

This guide will show you how to see family-related, private and professional relationships and their karmic aspects with renewed clarity.

The aim of this book is to give you deep insights into entanglements that lead to unhappy relationships. Here, you will find out how un-happiness is character-ised by the un-imaginable. You will get an overview of possible structures in your personal life history, ena-bling you to access a new ability to act which allows for personal freedom and also a new ability to achieve happiness in romantic relationships.

This guide takes a serious look at the true roots of deep despair felt by people injured by love. This is not possible without going deep to the basis of reality and personal responsibility. As a reward for your courage, I will lead you from the depths of inner turmoil, confu-sion and mental injuries to a safe path of change in your personal story and into a new quality of life.

This may open a new space for a fulfilled, joyful love relationship, which also includes a worthy place for tenderness and a mindful, sensual and erotic encounter in sexuality.

Now it's up to you to decide whether you are ready to take the necessary steps!

If you want to understand and change relationships, you cannot avoid confronting the misfortune that also comes with them.

Difficulties in relationships are often experienced as a personal defeat for which you blame yourself, others or fate. Perhaps you are familiar with the feeling of having drawn a "blank" yet again or suddenly finding yourself on your own again, quite out of the blue. But what are the dynamics that affect relationships, when even happy dating can come to an abrupt end? How can we deal with the variety of questions concerning relationships and find good solutions? The guide "The Secret of Karmic Relationships" gives you clear and easily comprehensible answers to these and many other questions.

The complex connections in partnerships and other relationships have probably never been described in such a comprehensive, clear and concise way before. Here, a lot of mysteries will be solved that have already given many people sleepless nights, in one lifetime or more.

As the author of this book, I would like to take this opportunity to introduce myself. This will help you to understand why I feel that I am qualified to provide you with this guide.

I have been fascinated by relationships since my early youth, which is why – despite my technical vocational training and my own company in this field – I followed my desire to gain further qualifications in the area of life counselling. This led me to start a private advisory practice a few years later and by now I have acquired over twenty-five years of experience.

Information on basic and advanced training in this field is intended for your orientation only.
For me, it was obviously necessary to follow all these pathways on which we have perhaps even met before. For you, this may mainly provide an indication that this guide is based on ethical, personal experiences and has been developed over many years.
During this time, I discovered and documented certain patterns in relationships and researched the backgrounds of difficulties and "misfortunes" back to their origins. My own life also brought many therapy-resistant mysteries which needed to be solved. All this led to the creation of a practical handbook which contains lots of checklists, a step-by-step guide and proven advice. With a number of exercises in the practical part you will receive a universal guide that will help you recognise, understand and change everything that has a burdening, stressful or unhappy effect on relationships.

This guide isn't just for all those people who always wanted to know what a karmic relationship is, it also reveals secrets that are wholly unknown even to experienced advisors, therapists and mediums!

Here, more questions will be answered than you have ever asked yourself about love, unhappy relationships, partnerships and sexuality. Among other things, the secrets of forbidden love, karmic love, karmic entanglements and dual souls will be revealed. Whether it's phenomena in relationships, physical symptoms or stubborn success blockages: many issues will appear in a completely new and clear light here.

Armed with this knowledge you will save yourself a fortune on courses, consultants, seminars and therapies that cannot help you because their providers have no experience with the complex cause-and-effect correlations in relationships.
This practical guide will give you all the answers to your questions and problems you need in order to regain solid ground under your feet again, even in crisis situations. Perhaps you would like to find out what some of the first readers of the PDF edition thought of it.

First reader opinions on the guide to karmic and other relationships.

I was very impressed by this extremely comprehensive read! Your recommendation to leave a certain time interval between reading the individual chapters so that the acquired knowledge can be applied more effectively to one's own situation is more than useful.

There were however some parts I personally could not take anything from. I would nevertheless recommend reading it, I had plenty of those truly interesting aha-moments.
Many thanks!
Rosstal, 13/02/2013, Betti Drechsler

I think your book is incredibly comprehensive, thorough and competent.

I was rather disorientated reading the first half. Even though I kept reading, it was all somehow abstract for me.
In retrospect I understand this part as the introduction. Actually, the book ceased to be something vague for me from the chapter "Trauma" in the second part: I felt it was applicable to me and to my life and therefore really exciting.
I found many answers to questions I had never asked myself consciously, but which are of great importance to my spiritual development. I think the practical part is especially great and incredibly useful!
Consequently I regard your book as a terrific gift! It has made me wonder whether I am actually conscious of which side I stand on.
I have been provided with specific tools and I am deeply touched and inspired to work with them. I am full of deep reverence for your knowledge and generosity!
In gratitude,
Berlin, October 8, 2012, Agnieszka Malkinska

The guide *"The Secret of Karmic Relationships" is clear and easy to read. This handbook is not one-sided but takes into account all aspects as a whole. Especially if you are also already familiar with literature by Brian L. Weiss and Trutz Hardo, "The Secret of Karmic Relationships" is a perfect supplement to these works.*

For my part, I can see myself very well in some chapters of the reading material mentioned above and I can therefore confirm many of the approaches therein. I especially liked the "Exercises To Clear Up Your Relationships", with the main focus on the "revocation of all bonds to death, dying and the dark side of life", "revocation of black magic" as well as "dissolution of eternal bonds between people" and, above all, the "ritual of forgiveness in order to clear up the past and the future". The guide is very detailed, clear and easy to apply because it explains the complex issues of partnerships and other relationships very precisely. It "helps in a pleasant way to regain the ground under your own feet".
In my opinion, really highly recommended!!!
25/10/2012, Daniela Ehing

Dear Bernd,

I started to read your book in the early evening yester-day and arrived on the last page at 11:15pm. You see, I simply could not stop reading. And this morning I still felt deeply affected by what I had read, because it is so full of truth. Your book has really moved me very much. You actually succeeded in creating a book which has never existed in this form before and which will certainly be helpful to many people. My compli-ments!!! I am full of appreciation. What you wrote about forgiveness touched me very deeply – the en-counter between perpetrator and victim.

An important part of your book is also sexuality. I have learned a lot from it! You also succeeded brilliantly in bringing its "dark sides" into a clear context with trau-ma. This will help people affected by this to achieve AHA-experiences (if they can open themselves to the truth). In any case, this is also very important infor-mation for (sexual) therapists! I have read about your own personal concerns in so many passages of your book that it's astonishing how you managed to show traumatic experiences and their consequences so ac-curately and to give courage and hope at the same time. And always with a touch of humour, which makes reading a pleasure. I hope that my reader's opinion will be able to contribute to the success of your book.

For I wholeheartedly wish you this success – Your work really deserves it.

All the best

Hannover, 04/11/2012, Ingeborg Christiansen

Since I read your book, the circumstances of my life finally make sense. I have already been in the healing process for several years and must say that I have been going round in circles for some time. The reason is that I could only recognise the real causes with the help of your book. For example, why and how the past manifests itself in the present, why (until now!) my life has been this way (and no other) and that I can only live my life when I completely recognise and resolve the causes of the past – when I find myself.

Your book will be a valuable companion to me for some time – you are right when you say it needs to be read several times, in order to explain again and again what is happening in the present and to reflect on it. Thank you for this invaluable book, I will recommend it to others!
Berlin, 30/03/2013
Sincerely, A. Ckus

I dedicate this guide to the ability of every person to "move mountains" for love if necessary and to reveal even the most difficult mysteries.

I express my thanks to all the people who have never given up faith in love and in themselves, even in the greatest crises of their lives. That is why I have always felt – I am not alone with this.
From the bottom of my heart I want to thank my lovely initiator who has inspired and challenged me in a special way, for the extraordinary time I spent with her. Without her, this guide might never have been written.

This guide is also an expression of my past responsibility. It has been created in the search for answers to incredible events and karmic relationships in my life.

With this book I want to provide you with a relationship guide which can accompany you in your future life. Maybe I will be able to reach something inside you on the following pages that calls for a freedom that you might have already given up.

Do You Really Believe?

Do you really believe
I do not know
how it feels
to be left alone again,
suddenly,
in incomprehensibility –
beyond
all
beautiful feelings?

Frozen
in the middle of the heart.
Searching for answers
in the middle of nowhere
and knowing only one question –
why?

Do you really believe
I do not know
how deeply injured
and sore
all this feels?

Do you know
how it feels
to know more,
but not enough?

Do you know,
what life is like
for me
without you?

Believe me,
despite all the burdens
that you carry,
this is "only"
a part
of it.
Believe me,
one human being alone
can never
be guilty.

Do you know
how it feels
to be victim and perpetrator
and to have no way out,
not even rage;
to carry
all the responsibility
and to feel longing
yourself,
like a wolf?

And nobody there
to talk to,
like you,
who could understand it.

09/10/2007

Why "Karmic" relationships?

All relationships are mainly determined by two kinds of dynamics. Cause and effect. For millennia, the timeless view of these things has been described most aptly in Buddhist teachings as the cycle and law of KARMA. Since I am not aware of any scientific model which includes timeless responsibility for personal thoughts and actions in such a clear form, I deliberately decided to use the conceptual reference to the principle of KARMA.

But there is another reason why I speak of "karmic" relationships. In its original form, the spiritual concept of KARMA clearly bases human existence on the validity and law of the "cause + effect" principle. Consequently, KARMA arises from a law, not from some random and unpredictable stroke of fate or the whim of a punitive "God".

The essence of this "spiritual" concept is the reference to the more scientific facts and the observation of cause and effect. Since many, even "spiritual" people, live in effects, without being able to establish a reference to the true causes, for me the "spiritual" model of KARMA establishes helpful ties to modern scientific and therapeutic procedures.

Not least, the "karmic" in the title of this guide creates room in a unique way for one of the best known and nonetheless most mysterious phenomena since the dawn of mankind. You might have guessed it already. It is love.

In the sense of this guide, "karmic" refers to a cycle of cause and effect which again and again leads to seemingly unsolvable conflicts at relationship level.

Many people do not understand their fate. They are often considered incurable or branded as crazy if they tell their story to someone else. Many people get no real help from conventional medicine, scientific methods or psychological counsellors. That's why those affected tend to search for answers using "spiritual" and "esoteric" methods. I have had the same experience, and this is how we can learn. What perhaps distinguishes me from others is the fact that I have studied and applied many methods without bias and put them under very critical scrutiny.

I know what clients are talking about when they speak of information which they received by channelling, holotropic breathwork, Fogo Sagrado, matrix work, aura surgery, all kinds of medial or shamanic sessions, astrological or numerological analysis, satsang, psycho kinesiology or regression. I know the limits and possibilities of many methods. Among other things, I am trained as a channel medium and a reiki master and have gained a lot of practical experience working as an esoteric life advisor and reincarnation therapist for many years. I have worked as an avatar trainer and I am trained in NLP. Please do not worry if you have never heard about any of this before. It has not helped me sufficiently to answer the essential questions of my own life, but I would simply like to reassure you that the content of this book reflects the essence of many methods as well as my own personal experiences, before you start to invest time and money in this guide.

I have always followed the feeling of open life questions to the bottom. I have regarded all my training as a starting point and pre-education but never as the final wisdom.

I would like to ask you to approach the information provided in this guide in the same way. Why is that important for you at this point? I have always found it helpful to expand the intellectual framework if the answers to certain life questions remained elusive. Even quantum physics begins to discover chains of influence that are still completely unknown to other scientific areas. It is important that we do not lose the connection to the present life and also establish it again and again in a therapeutic context. The question is always with what responsibility and purpose I use or explore a particular method. The seriousness and depth to which I dedicate myself to a particular subject is also important. That's why I use the term "deep life counselling" as the concept for my practice.

Many users misuse regression as escape projections for example or for time travel (according to my instructor). The therapeutically necessary connection to the present and the current life is often not made. That way all the "bad" can remain in the past and leave the ideal world illusion untouched in this life. It is often difficult to establish a reference. Even I could not always completely manage to establish a reference to some issues. The open questions were an incentive for me to do more research, not only to find answers but also to develop my therapeutic skills and options.

When I refer to information from regression in this guide, I thereby ask you to understand this as a summary of therapeutic work that is neither completed nor provides a complete picture. I would merely like to use this to give you a brief insight into this methodology and my therapeutic roots. This way you might get an idea of how this book has developed and why I work as a trauma therapist today.

As a person and a therapist I am not afraid of you coming to me and telling me that you can see the souls of deceased people. I know what you are talking about and I will take you seriously. As a child this scared me pretty badly because I was harassed by "souls" searching for my help. Back then I did not know what to do. I had a connection to "something" that I did not understand, and help in such matters was unattainable in my childhood. This personal helplessness and perception of visible and invisible relationships to people's souls led me to develop a curiosity which continues unabatedly to this day: the curiosity to recognise relationships in which we live, to understand and to change them for the better.

There was a time when no doctor or scientist had any idea about viruses, much less that someone could make them visible. There was a time when people were burnt for the fact that they could help in cases where doctors were at their wits' end. Perhaps one day, Kirlian photography or another method will be developed to the extent that the "souls" of deceased people or their energy bodies can reliably be made visible. Maybe one day technologies and scientific explanations will surface that will give practical, useful help for everything that "light workers" have already been doing for decades.

For me personally, ways of thinking and acting which are limited to this one life are too simplistic. A "spiritual" concept that supports me mentally in breaking away from the widespread "après moi, le déluge" mentality, seems to me to be much more helpful. However, please be aware that this is only a concept. The terms used in this book such as Karma, psyche, soul, spirit, past lives, psychological splitting and others are also only intended as models. On the following pages, I have used the terms / models / concepts which are commonly applied in the vernacular and society as well as in a scientific-therapeutic context, even if I personally have my own issues with some of them. With this in mind, as the author, I would like to use some terms which you have probably heard or read already. Personally, I am not attached to any of these terms and would not like to see them made into a religion. Therefore, you can use one of your own definitions for the notions of "direction", "quality" or "vibration" suggested by me.

Does the soul, the mind or the psyche love, or only the physical heart? Such discussions can be conducted elsewhere.

With or without love. According to the principles of cause and effect, every person creates timeless chains of events with their actions or inactions. However, in the course of their history, human beings often lose track of the complex connections and implications of their actions. Above all, they lose access to the correct actions to step out of undesirable chains of events in the "here and now".

If you want to understand yourself in the mirror of your relationships and chains of events, it makes sense to rely upon a timeless view of things. In order to do this, you do not need to believe in previous or future lives. For some therapeutic colleagues, the spiritual context of my explanations might be a thorn in their sides. But to be honest, I did not write this guide for them, although I am certainly pleased about benevolent interest from these circles.

I like to pick people up from the point they're at, and similar experiences in the so-called "spiritual" area are a helpful bridge for an honest encounter. The clarity I have gained from a multitude of such experiences underlines the credibility of my therapeutic invitation to gradually leave "spiritual" or other vanishing points.

The secret of karmic relationships has also emerged from my personal history and thus enabled me as the author to integrate my roots, experiences and references into this book and its title.
From what I know now, I was already born with "burnout". After that, the real difficulties began. Even now, while writing these lines, I still struggle to explain in terms of scientific criteria alone how I was able to sur-

vive this period. With all due respect for science and reputable therapeutic analysis – it was not available to me at the most difficult time of my life. And I doubt that it could have helped me even then.

> **Our existence beyond concepts leads us to what moves us deep down in our hearts as human beings. It is there that we often discover contra-dicting, hurt and frozen feelings which are part of the un-freedom we experience on a relationship level as well.**

The secret of karmic relationships is a documentary about human entanglements and their causes. By incorporating timeless, karmic principles, the view opens up to solutions which can lead into a new freedom and clarity beyond conventional perspectives, not only in terms of love relationships.

From my own life story and practical work as a life counsellor and trauma therapist a unique way has developed to explore deeper connections. It has become clear that we can change impacts and life situations easier if we recognise, understand and comprehend broader connections in their entire dimension. Maybe the information and real-life examples provided on the following pages will help you to gain a more complete picture of your own life story.

30

This guide is not a substitute for psychiatric or medical treatment. The responsibility for use, implementation and application of any information and exercises provided here rests solely with you. Terminology used in this book is only meant as a commonly known point of reference for certain qualities of experiences.

I would be delighted if something you found in this book helped you to create a nicer version of your life.

A professional background for you:

Brief Information on Regression

Corresponding to their age, everyone has problems that appear to be very difficult or intractable. When we reach a higher age bracket, we are usually able to recognise the challenges of previous years and often see a variety of solutions.

Unresolved conflicts and painful experiences are often suppressed during the phase of experience. Later they cannot be remembered consciously as the cause of disturbances which continue to burden us.

Reincarnation therapy uses the knowledge that we are always wiser afterwards than we were before in order to clear up and dissolve repressed conflicts from the past, from earlier ages and "previous lives", by way of regression.

The term "past life" primarily serves as a model to enable easy immersion into past structures. An important part of serious reincarnation therapy, as I have learned it at least, is the interpretation of the information thus obtained. The real purpose of this method is the targeted support of clients in order to learn and analyse the parallel experience in this life relating to that core information.

Reincarnation therapy does not require a belief in rebirth (reincarnation), even if that is included in this model. Being open to this process allows a playful access to important information that ordinarily remains closed to us.

Nowadays I use an even more effective method than reincarnation therapy. You will find out more about it in this guide.

The knowledge and information I would like to convey to you in this guide essentially consists of three parts. Each part is an important phase for the initiation and support of a process of change which only becomes possible through the deeper understanding and timeless view of chains of events.

In order to be able to change relationship situations permanently, it is helpful to be aware of these phases. The key to change is your willingness to go through these phases consciously.

Part I
– Recognise the pattern

Part II
– Understand the connections

Part III
– Break free from burdensome entanglements

Each chapter is like a step into a new level of consciousness.

At each level, this guide opens the opportunity to you to expand your views and experiences on a particular topic.

Even just the process of reading sets free certain impulses which you perhaps won't transfer into consciousness as knowledge until you get to the next chapter or the chapter after that.

With each change of your perception you gain a deeper understanding of yourself and others. Your picture becomes clearer and more comprehensive. With each openness to enter new levels in your consciousness you come closer to clearing up your relationships. With this in mind, I would like to invite you and ask you to follow the structure of the chapters without bias. If you trust me and follow me, everything will suddenly appear logical to you from a certain point in the book. In this moment of great meaningfulness and clarity you will have accepted the key to your personal freedom. If you feel it, then this book has served its purpose.

This guide is designed so that you can read it time and time again. With each "round", you will discover new things and recognise other contexts. Maybe you will ask yourself at one point or another whether the information there had already been mentioned before.

"The Secret of Karmic Relationships" is a journey through human and emotional entanglements to new perspectives and possibilities in order to pass through gates to freedom. I hope you have fun rediscovering your life/lives in the mirror of these realisations.

Important advice on the use of the seven steps:

Since I do not know your life situation, your problems and questions, this guide is written like a kind of checklist. Each part contains a possible step to solve your personal life situation.

Not every point on the checklist will necessarily apply to you personally.

If you feel that you do not know what a chapter or section is about, just read on. Do not linger with explanations which might seem stodgy, boring or too "esoteric" to you at the moment. You can rightly assume that exactly this issue is very interesting to other readers.

For a technician who carries out a car inspection, those points on his checklist where he does not notice any defects are also "uninteresting". Without a checklist he would however regularly fail to spot important issues (brake pads, hydraulic oil ...).

Therefore relax, go on reading nonetheless and proceed to the next step.

After all, the aim is for us to figure out together where in your life there might be any "snags". That's well worth investing a little patience and time. Above all, it is helpful to use a systematic approach developed from experience and proven in counselling practice.

You can also use this guide as a reference book and read those sections first that particularly catch your attention in the chapter overview.

If you have gone through all seven steps and could not find a reference to your life circumstances at any point of the checklist, I congratulate you on your happy life.

However, if you do not feel entirely happy and found the entire book stodgy and boring, you have most likely fallen into the "It's not as bad as all that" trap. Perhaps you know this better from everyday life or from your friends' examples. Almost daily you feel annoyed by the broken tiles in the bathroom, the yellowed wallpaper or the threadbare carpet. Anybody could just deal with it "but actually, it's not that bad". You probably ought to know that there are parts in every one of us that are not interested in the truth or real answers. You will learn more about that in part 5.

These parts are very creative in finding excuses, diversions and ruses. Anything you do not want to hear, see, read, or feel, is cleverly censored. This way, a film, a book or a person quickly becomes "stupid" and we no longer have to consider what we have heard, seen, read or felt. More often than not there are fears behind these protective mechanisms. Among others, fear of the effort which has to be made in order to change things.

So trust those parts of you which have led you to this book. These "healthy" parts inside you would like to bring you into contact with certain information. Otherwise you would not be reading these lines now. So be careful and watch out for the pitfalls of your "counter-party"! I know that this guide is not perfect. Perhaps it reflects our life better that way. Do not let the style or the language of this book stop you or irritate you either. Of course you personally are only interested in finding your way out of the "deadlock" you might currently be in. Since this book was written for a variety of people, it may well be that the aha-moments for your type of "deadlock" will only appear once you get to part 5.

The key to your secret is ready. I have described the way to it with the means available to me. Everything else is up to you now. Good luck.

PS: Before you go on a long trip, you should always examine your luggage carefully. I know that's boring and not nearly as much fun as the view over the Atlantic Ocean from the airplane. From my own experience I know that certain things do not belong into your luggage if you want to have happy relationships. You would not even be able to recognise your soul mate / your dream partner with certain items in your "baggage", even if that person was already by your side. That's why I ask you to see the first chapters as your steps through the check-in process.

Pictorial representation might make it easier for you to follow each step. Let's suppose that you have ten spiders, a rat and a skunk in your hand luggage. Can you imagine that it would massively affect the number of passengers who would want to share a cabin with you and voluntarily take a seat next to you?

So as your relationship coach, I therefore attach great importance to systematic "baggage checks". And maybe you will give me a funny look when I ask you various questions such as: Could it be that you have a "rat" in your "baggage"? Is it yours? Would you really like to keep it? I do not want to take away your beloved animals. It is up to you alone to decide what you would like to keep in your "baggage". If there are still ten spiders, one rat and one skunk at the end, it is pretty clear that you love special animals and your ideal partner should share this particular predilection. It would also be helpful in certain circumstances to choose a profession that allows you to enjoy many happy relationships with particular animals.

Precious Diamond

As I followed the tears,
I found the river,
and since I had lost
and given up everything
that had been important until now,
I let myself get carried away,
despite the risk
of drowning.

When I followed the river
between life and death,
I found a sea of tears
and in its depths
dark secrets
of times old and new.

I thus discovered
astounding answers
which I would have needed
much earlier,
but only later,
when the battle was lost,
I could find
in greatest willingness and humility,
the ability to do everything
to honour those Lost
in love.

For the immortal soul
every tear
is a precious diamond;
for us humans
terrible fate
only becomes valuable
when we accept it fully
and learn
to understand it
with our hearts.

Look deeper!

Part 1: The Secret Explosive of Each Relationship

Every relationship is a mixed unit with special dynamics, sometimes with a lot of dynamite.

In karmic relationships people frequently feel powerless and vulnerable - often a victim of circumstances. If you look deeper, you sometimes also recognise the victim on the other side. No matter what form you encounter in this life, you should know and recognise the most basic forms and motivations in order to better understand the part of your own victimhood. Why is that important? Unresolved victim-perpetrator-structures from your past work like explosives in any new relationship.

Perhaps you are already standing on the "sunny side" of life. Even so, you can still learn a lot about other people and their deeper relationship problems in this first part. Let me start with three principles:

Principle I
Victims are often closer to the operating table than to awareness.

Principle II
As long as we are unwilling to recognise and admit that and where we actually were or are the victims, we stay entangled with the perpetrator and live in victim-perpetrator-structures that sabotage and destroy our happiness over and over again.

Principle III
As long as we are unwilling to recognise and admit that and where we actually were or are the perpetrators, we stay entangled with the victims and with what made us a perpetrator and keep on living in victim-perpetrator/perpetrator-victim structures that sabotage and destroy our happiness over and over again.

People who start to understand these structures also start to understand relationship dynamics and their origins.

"Voluntary" Sacrifice

There is one type of victim which is not always anything to do with guilt or feelings of guilt, even if another form of guilt is sometimes made up for this way.

We always encounter "voluntary" victims in situations and circumstances that challenge us and cast doubt on our existing views of life. They serve us and others by making us think about their sacrifice in order to explore its sense, which is often seemingly missing. For example, children dying early help their parents to think about death, the meaning of life, birth, a possible life after death, reincarnation and everything that is to do with human existence. This way, the child's soul gives the parents a chance to live a more conscious life.

Point of Reference:
Things that seem pointless to us
are merely things the meaning of which we have
not yet recognised.

Among the "voluntary" victims there are souls who pay off an old debt this way as well as those who take on this role out of pure compassion.

Without the acceptance of a "life after death" and re-birth, "voluntary" sacrifices can rarely be understood. If you do not personally believe in these things but come across them nevertheless, take this as a gift that also carries a challenge which you do not have to accept. However, if you are confronted with this subject again and again, I can only recommend that you open your-self to the issue and deal with it despite all your reservations. Above all, use this opportunity to allow yourself to expand, to change and to transform your previous experiences and your understanding of dif-ferent issues with new impressions and different insights.

"Voluntary" victims consciously enter a situation in order to serve others. However, they do this WITHOUT any expectations.

> **If our heart opens itself in love and we feel that we can learn something from the sacrifice of another person, then we have most certainly recognised the gift of a "voluntary" victim. We feel gratitude, love, sympathy and inner strength. The "victim" follows their destiny and we ours.**

"Involuntary" Sacrifice

There is a type of victim which we recognise specifically by the "involuntary" sacrifices which the people around them make for them. That's why I have named the second type of victim after this characteristic.

As a general rule, "involuntary" victims and "martyrs" unconsciously bring about situations for their own benefit. They then expect recognition, support and help from others.

Their "sacrifice" serves a personal purpose and is often a pure, unconscious self-punishing mechanism. Here, above all, the "victim" itself has to learn.

If a victim forces us into actions which are primarily based on feelings of guilt, a sense of duty, obligation and compassion, it is often a sign that we **serve the victims "involuntarily"**. When this happens, the feeling of love soon falls by the wayside. The situation weakens us. Deep inside, we wait until it is "finally" over, forgotten, finished.

Out of ignorance, we accept the challenge that the supposed victim itself does not want to face. We thus often rob other people of the learning experience they should gain from their own fate.

For example, if you let yourself be controlled by a sick or disabled person, you deprive them of the opportunity to grow up and take responsibility for their own life. At the same time, your belief that you are doing something good unconsciously probably serves you as an excuse for not facing up to your own learning task in this regard. "There is no way I can do that" and similar thoughts reflect your need for action which you do not dare to follow out of ignorance of the deeper questions of the meaning of fate. The victims we serve "involuntarily" refuse to take their destiny "into their own hands" in a creative way and to follow the challenges of life with self-responsibility and independence. The victims complain and ask for help from others. Anyone who gives them more than just help to help themselves carries the responsibility for impeding the development of another human being! Do **not always** take on more of your partner's burdens than you are happy to.

> **Point of Reference:**
> You recognise the "type of victim" not by their outward appearance, but especially by how the "victim" deals with their fate.
> Those who see themselves as victims often have not yet recognised their own perpetrator structure.

Even if someone has a causal responsibility for the "victim" – for example, a woman addicted to pills has a disabled child etc. – this person is not entitled to impede the development of the victim. Everyone has the right and the duty to develop their own creative ways which lead to greatest possible independence and an autonomous life. That is precisely the central challenge and learning task of each individual life.

Some people have consciously decided to take on bigger tasks. You therefore have to be very deliberate in your dealings with "victims". A guideline – for how you might accompany and support "victims" – should always be the desire to help people to help themselves.

You will meet the responsibility for personal "guilt" – regarding a victim – by carrying this "guilt" with dignity and avoiding false attempts to make amends.

Mixed Unit

In relationships we encounter other people in various victim-perpetrator and perpetrator-victim dynamics. When we get the chance to observe ourselves in a quiet moment and to question our actions honestly, we may become aware of situations where we had the feeling of not being quite ourselves. Our words or actions turned us into "perpetrators" and afterwards we didn't know how this could have happened. You might also have noticed a specific internal impulse to express "offensive words" which you did not follow but which has bothered you considerably. Or in an extreme case, you might even have noticed an impulse "to pick up a knife and stab" and to this day you ask yourself where that came from. Such things often remain our secret and our deepest distress because we do not know who we can talk to about it openly.

Point of Reference:

When it comes to impulses that try to push us in victim or perpetrator situations and do not fit with our own nature, structures taken from the family system often become apparent with which we are still entangled today.

Such unresolved symbiotic entanglements often lead to seemingly intractable conflicts and events in which we recognise ourselves as victims and perpetrators at the same time. Such influences regularly cause confusion, chaos and emotional distress in our relationships and partnerships. If such situations seem familiar to you, Part 5 in particular will give you more detailed information about such dynamics and the backgrounds of psychological entanglements that can affect several generations. Fortunately, the responsibility to deal with such challenges lies solely in your hands and gives you the opportunity to change something. It will be my pleasure to support you in breaking free from such dynamics and entanglements.

Hint:

Since most of our personality imprints arise from a phase of life in which we have not yet developed our own consciousness, it is almost impossible to figure out by ourselves which "harmful" external structures we have unconsciously adopted.

Note:
As long as we do not recognise and clear up our own victim-perpetrator-structures and related entanglements, they will always be apparent in our life- and love relationships as a disturbing, often divisive factor.

Victim as a Lead Role

There are people who are very successful in proving to other people that they are beyond help. According to the motto: "I am and will remain a victim, come what may. No one can bear me and love me."

Various things hide behind those often unconscious thought patterns and beliefs. Firstly, there is certainly a hope that lots of people will try it anyway. Because: "If someone managed to do it (which is almost impossible), I would at least know that someone is taking me seriously". Secondly, this obviously shows an injured person who thus far hasn't been able to decipher their own life plan from their past experiences in life. The major challenges of this interesting creation involve some elements that need to be considered and understood.

The seven "dangers" in this regard are:

1. That the person gets to the point where they like themselves so much in their role that they cannot give it up, even if the "Prince" or "Princess" has already stormed the "fortress".

2. That the person sinks into a very deep life crisis when time and time again they have to enjoy their success (in proving that nobody can stand them, etc.) lonely and alone. They experience their success as a failure because they have forgotten their original idea and basic concept.

3. Once the person has proven to the whole world that nobody can bear them, there is nobody left who might still prove the opposite.

4. That everyone recognises that this is someone who wants to be seen as an actor in the "victim role" - they refuse their approval or simply cannot applaud any longer because their hands are already sore from clapping.

5. That in his "victim role", the actor forgets that there are many other interesting roles in life for which he could apply as the lead actor. He basically keeps practicing for so long that one day he becomes the most perfect victim role actor in the world.

6. That the person considers this partial task and this role which is intended only as preparation to already be their life plan. They do not realise that other aspects – such as lightness and joy of life – are also waiting to be explored, just like the role of "perpetrator" in a positive sense.

7. That the true cause and personal distress which led to this survival structure will never be clarified.

Each life plan is different. Those who do not recognise or understand the victim role as just one of many possible starting points might well only concentrate on this experience for their entire lives. I hope you have already developed enough curiosity or boredom to explore other aspects of this "role".

On closer examination, the issue is more complex than it might seem at first glance. In its own way it contains everything that life has to offer, e.g.:

- How we act and how people act towards us, the background to victim-and-perpetrator structures, unclear victim experiences

- Live and let live

- Grief, injury and healing of emotions

- Confusion, despair and basic trust

- Desire to be loved and unconditional love

- Absolute privation and limitless abundance

- Loneliness and ability to be happy alone

- Guilt and forgiveness, redemption

It is no surprise that this enormous versatility makes the issue so popular. Millions of "students" have already chosen this programme. However, since study time is unlimited, they often stay with the simple victim aspects for too long. The real challenge however lies in recognising and understanding the higher reaching opposite poles and in integrating all aspects of these polarities.

Unsuspecting Victims

There are also victims who do not know or still do not accept that they have been victims. There are good reasons for this of course. Anything we do not know or do not want to admit does however block our insight into the causes and correlations of experiences which are still reflected as "misfortune" in our lives today. Perhaps it was the desire to lift the veil on your misfortune that led you to this book. I promise to lift this veil for you on the following pages as carefully and completely as possible.

Victims Live in a Constant Holding Pattern – And Not Always Their Own!

If we – consciously or unconsciously – live within victim structures, our lives are always missing something.

When "satisfaction" and "compensation" fail to materialise for victims, life usually becomes rather restricted. Unless we have an idea. This idea could lead to the insight and knowledge that:

- the feelings of being a victim do not "completely" belong to oneself

- other perspectives are possible

- many events can also provide positive learning experiences

- the fact that we feel that we are victims may not be anything to do with the current issue but rather with the background, life structures and conditions that have led to how we experience the current issue

The "bad" experiences of victims will not stop as long as they keep their victim mentality and reproachful attitude. Why is that? As long as we – consciously or unconsciously – wait for compensation and recognition of our "destiny" by others, our life is literally on hold. This holding pattern is dependent on how others react to us. The longer we live in this suspended state, the greater our anger with others will often become. This concentrated anger is often wrongly directed towards our partner, who in general is nothing to do with our still unresolved previous experience.

Point of Reference:
Truly happy people might wait for the metro but they most certainly won't wait for life. Unhappy relationships are often an indication of unclarified "victim structures".

True autonomy is the freedom to design our own lives, even if and especially in the absence of reactions by others!

Even in relationships, we constantly get into such "holding patterns" because the other... Here, clear agreements, clear messages and alternative independent action without reproach or blame are helpful if agreements or deadlines are not met! Do not let anyone put you on the bench and make you wait. Act.

If time after time you feel stuck in an inability to act, the first step you could take is to call it a "behaviour pattern" that you would like to change. But use your energy to clear up the true causes and do not try to change your partner's/your counterpart's behaviour pattern! Be grateful for the "symptoms", but please do not confuse them with the causes.

I would therefore like to invite you at this point to take a closer look at your "victim status" and your "willingness to make sacrifices" within your day-to-day relationships.

Note:
If we live our lives feeling that life still owes us something, we are, consciously or unconsciously, living in victim structures that are still unclarified.

Each "victim" has its "victim experience", which is typically dominated by aspects such as despair, hopelessness, subjugation and helplessness.

An insufficiently processed victim experience subconsciously often leads to a kind of inner victimhood. This is often associated with anxiety and the expectation of further unhappiness – "When will it happen again?" Until such victim mentality is clarified and resolved, the victim experience often has the effect of a kind of permanent magnet for similar experiences.

You can read more on that in Part 5.

Point of Reference:
As long as you live with a perhaps subconscious victim mentality or unprocessed victim experience, you will repeatedly face perpetrator structures in your life. If people often meet you with offensive words, you know what I mean. If threatening or violent partners are not unknown to you, you should take this issue seriously.

What Could You Learn for Your Relationships from This Part?

From this first part I would like you to learn one thing in particular:

If questions in life repeat, your answers can change.

Checklist for Part 1 – What Exactly Can You Do Right Now?

Step 1:

Clearing Up of Your Own Victim-Perpetrator-Structure

The preferred attitude in partnerships should be that of a loving person. The less relaxed and confident we are in seeing ourselves as part of a loving relationship (with ourselves and others), the more those hitherto unclarified victim-perpetrator-structures affect our lives. The following questions may be helpful in gaining awareness of these issues.

Questions to clear up your personal victim-perpetrator-structure:

- Are there situations or events in your relationships which render you speechless and helpless?

- Are there situations or events in your profession which render you speechless and helpless?

- Under what circumstances do you feel completely powerless?

- Is there anything in your partner's behaviour that "drives you nuts"?

- Does your superior's behaviour "drive you nuts"?

- Are there people or events that always make you feel entirely vulnerable and powerless?

- Is there something in your neighbour's behaviour that "drives you nuts"?

- What are the situations or events where you always feel yourself getting more stressed than would objectively be necessary and reasonable?

- Who are the people involved in these situations? Who comes to mind when you think about this?

- If you observed yourself acting in such a situation in a movie, which person would you most likely associate with your own behaviour?

- In what situations do you feel guilty?

- In what situations do you not live in truthfulness?

- In what situations do you shield, tolerate or submit yourself to perpetrators?

- In what situations do you sacrifice yourself?

Victim and Perpetrator

The misfortune
of being both victim
and perpetrator
sometimes falls
so deep
into our soul
that only
divine mercy and wisdom
can rescue us
from it.

We also tend to waste a lot of time trying to press ahead with the fulfilment of our own desires or to sabotage the wishes of others, often without properly considering spiritual and karmic aspects. This always leads to misunderstandings, confusion, despair and spiritual deadlocks.

For as long as you still consider yourself a victim on a relationship level, you have not yet integrated the healing aspects of this leaning task completely. Maybe the following information will help you to find a new access, since victims always have unfulfilled desires and some of our wishes have their origins in a curse or a magic love spell.

Why Wait Ten Years?
Laugh about it Right Now!

Part 2: Secret Knowledge

About Wishes and Curses
and the Biggest Mistake in History

The soul's starting point (its origin) is crucial in determining what it can or should do in order to achieve its goals!
The degree of karmic freedom or binding responsibility (guilt) is the key to understanding your personal experience with wishes, curses and intercessions.

Every relationship is unique in its history but in my experience, all karmic relationships have one thing in common: There are eternally binding energy structures which have their origin in powerful wishes, curses or other sometimes magical practices. People affected by this are often entangled in confusing feelings which they are not able to decipher by themselves. A specific example from my practice:

For a woman, a relationship with a married man was destined for failure from the very beginning. After the separation, she suffered for many years and concealed the fact that she'd had his child. Working through the karmic entanglement revealed that this man had destroyed the deeply loving relationship between the woman and another man in a previous life using a love spell, in order to win the woman for himself. Many lives with unhappy partnerships and confusing feelings followed, until in this life the woman started to decipher the origin of the karmic relationship patterns by regression. That way she could finally understand and resolve the unfortunate karmic fixation with a man who she had never really been in love with! And she also discovered her true, lost heart love again.

However, in order to fully clarify and understand such a relationship pattern, more steps are needed. The client's inner, mental image may also reflect a symbiotic entanglement with her mother's or grandmother's experiences, feelings and relationship patterns.

Wishes, Curses and Intercessions

Most wishes, curses and intercessions refer to health, worldly goods or an ideal partner. Despite sufficient literature and seminars, especially concerning abundance, consciousness of wealth and manifestations of desires, the principle seems to work chiefly for the authors and seminar instructors themselves. In my case it was quite the opposite for a long time, but that is another story.

Why does the manifestation of wishes not work in your case, despite you having done everything "right"?

If your wishes do not "work", "curses", magical bonds, ancient agreements, your own soul contracts or karmic patterns are standing in the way and are preventing them from working for all eternity or making them impossible at a particular point in time. If your ability to manifest desires and goals of all kinds is "disturbed", this might also be a clear indication of a traumatic childhood which you are no longer conscious of. I will go into the topic of TRAUMA in more detail later.

In general, **a wish** is a desire for a gift we want to receive.

A curse is the conscious or unconscious practice to wish that certain things will remain unattainable to somebody else or that something happens to them. It has the effect of spiritual poison on all levels of the person affected. The effect of a curse (malediction – all kinds of damage spells) depends on the spiritual power of the person cursing as well as their karmic imprint. In extreme cases, it can even entail death.

Now you might say: "I would never do that" and "In my case, something like that would never work" – Am I right? What point am I trying to make?

On the Biggest Mistake in History, Made by All People, Not Only Those Who Approach this Topic in a Spiritual Way!

Only because people's own wishes do not come true, most of them assume that their spiritual curses will not cause damage to other people either. Many people therefore give free rein to such thoughts and do not think about what "negative things" they are wishing on other people. And in any case, the other person does not deserve any different, do they?

Point of Reference:
"Negative" wishes are subject to completely different laws to "positive" wishes.

"Negative" wishes do not need any external rituals (candles, moon, other people's help) in order to work. However, external rituals can be additional boosters.

"Negative" wishes are effective even if they are spoken by people who are unsuccessful in making their own wishes come true!

This is because the dark side of the force – you could also call it demonic forces or **negatively program-ming energy structures** – quasi as subcontractors – automatically receives your instruction and carries it out as best as possible, depending on your "contract status". As a special service, "club" members' wishes will not only be read from their lips, but also straight from their thoughts. Terms of payment and type of in-voice settlement are different for each individual and dependent on the type of your "business relationship".

Only the eternal soul remains bound by this "business relationship", independent of the changing forms of dif-ferent incarnations – how could it be otherwise? Even if we leave aside the possibility of previous lives. You should know that your personal "debt" to the dark side of the force grows with each of your "curses" in this life. You remain in a timeless obligation with regards to this personal responsibility, even independently of other persons or organisations.

In such cases, the buyer always pays for delivery! You remain obliged to pay compensation, whether you believe it or not. Your bond with the dark forces grows stronger with each order. The collateral is always the freedom of your eternal soul.

The goal of the exercises in Part 7 is to regain this freedom and requires a new decision which you can make anytime.

Your only constant "obligation" towards the divine is the truth and unconditional love.

The truth as I have found out it is that every negative thought has an effect about "1,000 times" stronger than a positive wish for yourself. Every thought is a spiritually effective force which always reaches its goal. However, depending on your personal karmic history, your thought patterns develop different dynamics.

Especially in spiritually-oriented people who are working through their karmic history in this life, the common practices of wishes and positive thinking do not work at all or only very unsatisfactorily. This is usually due to previous bonds to the dark side of the force in this or past lives. Furthermore, it is also likely that there is a lack of karmic merit, humility, gratitude, etc., all of which would allow for the fulfilment of your desires at this point in time already.

You may have decided to devote your soul to the divine in this life, but divine blessing (abundance on all levels, etc.) can only be given to you in full if you make a new, conscious, clear and explicit decision about which side you are really on.

As long as "curses" still rise up inside you, you have not yet sufficiently understood parts of your karmic history. If that is the case, your divine being is not yet fully connected to unconditional love. You are basically sitting on the fence and the seduction of the dark side continues to tempt you with many "gifts" that are delivered immediately after ordering.

However, this does not mean that you have to suppress healthy impulses of rage or anger.

If necessary, give them room by using all legal means to provide truth and clarity. Your divine being's wisdom has more options than to simply employ the dark forces and to put itself on the same level as the others.

> **Point of Reference:**
> Your contracts with the "dark side" can very well be as old as the universe. For as long as they exist, a full life in new and divine freedom is not possible. For help, see "Revocation of black magic" in the exercises

Why does this "wishing stuff" work for other people then? There can be several reasons for that:

- The soul has desired the experience for this life that "all its wishes fulfil themselves"

- The person has gathered many karmic merits

- The person does not question the bond to the "dark side of the force".

- Those who are successful in "wishes" only serve to confuse spiritual seekers.

- Successful "wishers" use additional black magic practices, consciously or unconsciously.

- Wishes serve higher, ethical purposes and are for the benefit of a community

However, the big secret of really successful people is something entirely different.

All of them have a "Plan B" for the fulfilment of their desires. Here is a short version of that.

- Desires have to be formulated as realistic goals with achievable partial objectives as waypoints.

- It is necessary to determine in writing when (date) and with what particular measures, actions and verifiable partial steps the intermediate stage can be achieved.

- Similarly, intermediate steps are used to convert unplanned obstacles into further partial successes.

Since time and time again relationships are also about common desires that often remain unfulfilled, I will illustrate the issue with a specific example:

What are the chances of fulfilment here?

I should / would like to / could go on holiday! How often have you thought something like that?

Honestly? Experience and practice show:
This is not a goal, but in every sense and dimension (chronologically – time period and duration, geographically – place, financially – savings plan) an unspecified thought, the fulfilment chances of which are virtually zero.

How do you estimate the chances of the following "Plan B" concerning wish fulfilment?

Next year, from 1ˢᵗ to 7ᵗʰ May, I will go on holiday to Switzerland with my partner.

I am going to book the hotel in Bern this week.

From now on, I am going to save € 150 / month for that via standing order to a deposit account which I have opened specifically for this purpose.

I will also transfer my Christmas bonus to this account this year.

We have both already submitted our application for time off which has been approved.

Just thinking about it I can already smell the fresh air.

Note:
Wishes come true faster if we decide on a realistic itinerary with predictable and dated milestones along the way to our main destination. Important goals in a partnership should therefore be planned together!

If scientists are right, the time we feel is going to pass by even faster for us. This is not because of our age but because of the permanently increasing speed the earth moves at. This is called accelerated earth rotation.

That's why you need a specific "Plan B" to achieve your desires and goals:

1. Write down one to three goals for this year which are important and realistic to you.

2. Define up to ten feasible milestones for each goal and set (in writing) a particular date for completion of each of the partial tasks. Is the goal not reachable in ten steps, it is too broad. Redraft it so that another partial goal is reachable in ten steps.

3. Concentrate on the respective next step you need to work on and tick it off solemnly once you have completed it.

4. Reward yourself each time you have completed a partial task (go for a walk or a meal, to the sauna, cinema or relax reading a book, ...)

5. If every month you fulfil a subtask for each of the three goals, you have an average of ten days for each of these sub-steps.

6. That leaves you a month for holidays (reward / halfway point) and a month as a reserve buffer zone for unexpected obstacles.

7. Whether it's work or pleasure: It is always a joy to achieve goals together when each partner in the relationship takes responsibility for doing so.

Perhaps you would like to give this a go. You have to be precise and determined every time! You also have to accept responsibility for your own personal unfulfilled desires before they mutate into explosives within your relationship.

Further education is another way to achieve the fulfilment of your wishes:

Recommended audiobook: T. Harv Eker, *Secrets of the Millionaire Mind*

This could easily be the best investment of your life. Among other things, the book contains tips on simple, efficient money management.

Intercessions

Put simply, intercessions are **positively formulated wishes for other people** (souls, beings, animals ...) which we direct to a divine source, selflessly, out of compassion and in deep, unconditional love.

Traditionally, intercessions have the "character of a prayer" if they are directed to a force or level which is not visible to us. They also contain an "application", where a good word is put in with a third party. The purpose is often a request for healing, rescue from emergency situations, warding off or mitigation of someone's destiny, help and guidance in seemingly hopeless situations.

This form of wishing is also subject to its own laws.
Intercessions are a holy, powerful key to divine freedom.

Hint:
Do not worry about the fact that visible results are not always achieved on an earthly level! Divine grace works beyond our human time perception.

A mature soul develops a natural desire to proffer intercessions. This often contributes to a part of the karmic balance in a natural way. Often a seeker's wishes are only fulfilled when the seeker steps beyond individual wants and desires and looks at the big picture in a healthy way and puts it into a new perspective. On this level of being, many old, unfulfilled wishes come true by themselves.

Again and again, major misunderstandings arise in interpersonal relationships and partnerships as well. In the following chapters we will analyse this in more detail.

Hints for re-thinkers, lateral thinkers, creative thinkers and reflective thinkers

You can easily tell the quality of your wishes, curses and intercessions from the quality of your partnerships and other relationships. If you understand this principle, you will also find it easier to see through the real intentions of particular people, politicians, groups, associations, parties, governments and so on. Simply take an unbiased look at the results, the present, the direction and the current situation. Then, take a look at the people who carry the main responsibility for these things. What sort of desires might be driving them if the results make sense from their point of view?

How do you feel about this? What direction are your life and your family's life moving in?

Consider what you yourself do and what you perceive in other people as an arrow shooting into the future. What trajectory is it following? What desire is it driven by? Which objective does the shooter serve? Do you perhaps want to change the direction but do not yet know how?

This guide will in any case massively expand your possibilities.

In order to clear up any form of relationship, you also need the courage to ask uncomfortable questions. As a thrifty taxpayer, for example, I have the right and the duty to ask questions about the permanent burden of government debt. Perhaps you have also done that before. If we dare to ask uncomfortable questions, we should however not make the mistake, for example, to consider the politicians stupid because we do not immediately understand their obvious plan for deliberate state indebtedness and impoverishment of the people! Here too, courageous questions lead to faster results. Who might have an interest in this? What leads to such a great desire? How about hate? Who could have such hatred for Germany? Why do politicians serve this goal? Do not worry. This book is not political. I just want to help you to expand your horizon and to develop alternative questions for all of your relationships. Some people, families and interest groups work on the realisation of certain desires for many decades and generations.

How good is your stamina? What is your biggest desire?

I know that you can get mischievous delight out of always thinking of new and creative curses for people who so obviously deserve it. But I also know that the seed of your curses will bear fruit in your own relationships and your further life. There are also individuals who are intent on always entangling others in new, destructive chains of events. From some individuals' perspectives this has the advantage that everyone who accepts such "invitations" or is entangled into them by subtle force, increasingly deviates from the possibility of personal freedom and autonomy. Since you have practically booked me as a kind of personal relationship coach by purchasing this guide, I see it as my duty to draw your attention to these issues as well as to possible doors to freedom. Far be it from me however to judge your personal lifestyle.

What Could You Learn for Your Relationships from This Part?

I would like you to take the following from this second part:

- With each "negative wish", you, as the commissioning party, accept the karmic and timelessly effective responsibility for all consequences of that negative wish.

- Through the act of "voicing a negative wish", you, as the commissioning party, enter a timeless relationship with the person the curse is directed at.

- As long as parts of your history are obscured by "karmic" shadows cast by your own, still effective curses, every one of your other relationships will always be affected by the cool touch of this dark shadow.

- Intercessions work by the power of selflessness and the force of unconditional love, even if they are expressed by people who apparently have no success with wishes they make for themselves!

Checklist for Part 2 – What Exactly Can You Do Right Now?

Step 2

Clearing Up of Your Relationships Linked by Negative Wishes

Write down what comes to your mind spontaneously while reading the following question:

Who have you ever cursed, damned, linked to your negative wishes or allowed to be linked by third parties? This is about an unbiased understanding of actions with which you created new causes, the long-term effects of which you cannot fully comprehend. The reasons play as little a role at the moment as the method of execution. Whether it was done in thoughts or spoken out loud, straight to the face or from another continent – it is about the action itself. I can assure you from my experience that each form has triggered a chain of events.

Simply write them all down one after the other on a separate list. If you still remember the nature of your negative wish or the damage spell you ordered, just write it in the right hand column, next to the appropriate person.

It could look like this for example:
PERSON – desire/negative thought

- the BMW driver who drove on the A81 motorway last year - "cursed his bones"

- the kids who play ball against the garage - that they get tired soon

- the neighbour who always takes a shower at night - wished "gout" on him

- my boyfriend who has left me – wished for him to die

- my girlfriend who has left me - wished that she would never get pregnant

- the woman my boyfriend has left me for - that she may lose all her hair

- myself, because last month I... – that I never manage it

- my boss who fired me - that he goes bankrupt soon
- ...

Keep adding to your list over the next few days, whenever anything else comes to mind.

At the moment, you do not have to do anything else with it. The following parts will help you to become more aware and get a deeper insight into the cause + effect principle and theory. In the exercise part you can use your new awareness to go back to the list, if you would like to follow the recommendations there.

Intercession for another person

As a second step in this chapter, I would like to invite you to ask for a blessing for someone else. Direct your intercession at a universal, higher, "divine" entity. In such cases, I often use the term "divine source".

For example, ask this universal divine "entity" on behalf of a particular person:

- to give him/her special protection, help, support

- for fast healing/recovery

- for rescue out of distress

- that everything goes well for her/him

- that her/his fields are blessed in a special way

- that her/his harvest is the best it's been in years

- that her/his children are always safe

- that risky plans towards a good cause will succeed

- …

You can pray for a person who is particularly dear to your heart or who you love very much.
It can be a "poor soul" somewhere near you or further afield. To start with, choose a person who you really want better things for than they are experiencing right

now and where your wish for them comes from deep in your heart.

If you can't think of anyone, you are very welcome to start with me. I could do with it. At this point, it is important to me that you get into action and simply do it. This is the only way for this experience to turn into a good habit.

If this is new to you, you probably will not notice much in the beginning. Over time, you will however notice a clear difference when you express an intercession from the bottom of your heart. Maybe it will even surprise you how clearly you can sometimes feel that your wish of blessing has been delivered successfully. Even if you never feel anything, it always "works".

The ideal partner
recognises
in the other person
a mirror
of themselves
and
does not break it

- 01/07/1996 -

Who does not wish to have their ideal partner by their side? However, there are always big gaps between desire and reality.

This prompts the legitimate question: Which ideal does our partner actually correspond to?

Part 3: The Ideal Partner – Mirror of the Subconscious

Insights from a spontaneous and unprepared expression of desires with regards to your ideal partner (man/woman of your dreams) must be split into two columns:

- positive qualities, character features which he/she should have, must meet, and the additional listing of

- negative qualities, character features which he/she absolutely must not have.

On closer inspection you will usually notice clear parallels to the way we have experienced our parents in positive and negative ways.

Things that we have experienced as positive from our father, our mother and other close contacts in our childhood automatically become the measure for expectations we have from our partners (present + future).

We seek a partner who represents a combination of all the positive qualities our parents had, but without any of the negative features we experienced from our father, mother or other close contacts in our early childhood.

Most people project these experience patterns on their partners without reflection. The reason why they usually correspond to the exact opposite of all our expectations is that childhood experiences have been repressed and left unprocessed. That is why we sub-consciously gravitate towards people who confront us with those suppressed issues as a mirror so often that we at last face up to them consciously (law of rhythm).

Each partner thus primarily serves as an aid in processing unresolved, suppressed experiences. They always represent the part in us that we have not realised in ourselves yet.

Also read more on this in Part 7: "A partner like my fa-ther – like my mother"

Love is
zest for life,
love is
lightness,
to love means
to let go –
everything else
is a projection
of our ego.

The prerequisite for really meeting our ideal partner and also for entering into a relationship with them is that we have first realised and lived all those positive aspects in ourselves which we expect to find in our partners.
Furthermore, it is also necessary for us to consciously understand and clear up all aspects which we associ-ate with negative experiences. This is usually only

possible by working through our relationships with our parents and other important contacts.

Through our partner, we always get the opportunity to re-examine our own positions and to reconsider our values because everything that strikes us about their behaviour mainly concerns us (resonance principle) and often reminds us of things that we considered closed and dealt with a long time ago. Moreover, we always judge their behaviour according to the filter of our past experiences and prejudice. Since many people confuse the symptoms (relationship issues) with the causes (unresolved personal issues) out of ignorance, they often spend decades living in seemingly intractable conflicts and repeated, unhappy relationships.

Personal destiny leads to feelings of unhappiness in relationships if your own life story is defined by deep emotional injuries which are not yet fully resolved.

An Example of the Consequence of a Negative Experience

What does a woman, whose former partner did not come back after popping out to get some cigarettes, think when her new partner says to her in the evening, "I'm just going out to get some cigarettes"?

What is the new partner to do with her old experience? How often does the new partner actually have to "come back" before this basically neutral process of getting cigarettes does not trigger any emotional connections with the negative experience in the woman anymore? – Once, a hundred or a thousand times?

A rule about negative experiences:
A negative experience cannot simply be wiped out by experiencing the same situation with a positive experience if the reason for the negative experience has not been understood. On the contrary, each identical, positive experience will in some form always be a reminder of the hitherto unresolved negative experience.

Due to a lack of understanding of these correlations, some people therefore even keep away from such "positive" experiences because they ultimately "make" them (depending on the severity and degree of the negative experience) go through the pain triggered by the memory of that experience again and again.

What does your partner remind you of?

Are there any "positive experiences" you are avoiding today?

Do you live in a partnership in which your partner always hides away in this protective manner?

Affected couples often live in long distance relationships or have separate apartments for many years. That way it is possible for the man or the woman to avoid the painful pressure of the positive experience as soon as it becomes too strong. If required, the man or the woman can retreat back into their protection zone which is still necessary for survival. This requires an enormous amount of tact, patience and understanding from the other partner. Here, trust will grow fastest if the "abandoned person" does not take the process personally and avoids wanting to treat the other. Independent, neutral counselling by a third party is very helpful in these cases, ideally before it comes to a permanent separation due to the great pressure of the positive experience.

Memory Effect

A great deal of attention should always be given to this memory effect in life. It leads us to issues that we have not yet sufficiently processed. The better we comprehend the reasons in our own life why we associate various things with negative feelings, the less our partner will have or need to have negative characteristics. All the negative and suppressed experience patterns always come back to us in the form of other people, like a boomerang. Thus, a partner is always a mirror of ourselves.

90

A Retrospective View – the Childhood

It is very helpful from today's perspective to ask ourselves what we perceived as a child, how we perceived it and why. Because as children, we inevitably have a very one-sided view which often cannot withstand an evaluation and review from today's perspective. That means that many things which we saw as negative in our parents we can judge more objectively now. On conscious reflection, many of those things were actually done in our best interest for example. By recognising this fact we can dissolve negative aspects and judgments or convert them into positive insights. By doing so, we of course also become freer in the relationship with our partners because their behaviour triggers fewer negative associations (memory effects) in us and we can therefore see them more objectively. – **"When two do the same thing, it is far from being identical"**.

Of course it may also be that – when analysing our parental image – we no longer consider some of the things we had perceived as positive as children to be desirable behaviours today or we even recognise negative aspects in them. In this case, we should not devalue or question the positive experiences of our childhood because they did serve us well after all. On the other hand this also teaches us a lesson for the future, to sometimes question things that appear beneficial to us at first glance. This is important not only for partnerships but for our whole life.

At times it may be easier to come to terms with "negative" (not understood, unresolved) aspects of the past when we learn to understand that we rated all information and experiences from the perspective of our own needs as a child. The primary objective is always to achieve an understanding of deeper connections in our own "karmic" history. Sometimes this also means to develop justifiable anger at our parents' immoral behaviour and to gain a reasonable distance in this relationship. In gratitude for the fact that this life has been given to us, we should open ourselves to all the challenges and responsibilities that it involves and take sole responsibility for them.

For example, those who spend their lives clinging to accusations against their parents, reveal their reluctance to act independently and creatively and to take responsibility for themselves.

Such people waste their lives because all their strength and personal development remain tied up with these accusations. On this basis, any partnership will of course also be full of accusations, passivity, disease, sorrow, lack of vivacity, unhappiness, jealousy and unkindness, to name but a few symptoms. Frequently these unclarified, unresolved aspects find their expression in over-activity in directions devoid of meaning.

Expectations of the Partner and Others

Many people expect their partner to change according to how they want them to be. They do not realise that they need to examine their own standards, prejudices and moral concepts in the first place as well as to confront suppressed experiences from the past. Thus a large number of people in our society spend all their lives waiting for other people to change and even reward themselves with a medal for their "patience". True to the motto: "I am the cheese, but it's the others that stink".

> **T h o s e who speak of love
> mostly only mean
> the expectation of others
> to be loved by them.**

Processing of the Parental Relationship

Since the most crucial influences always stem from our childhood, processing our parental relationship is the most important step to a fulfilled partnership. It is particularly important for us to break free of any guilt projections on third parties. This often allows existing relationships that are close to failure to achieve a whole new freedom. One's own point of view is always the essential factor here.

Once you have re-evaluated your personal, suppressed aspects, you may recognise that you have the "wrong" partner for your future. However, through your own transformation, you may understand why this is so and become open and ready for a new dimension of partnership. Always keep in mind:

- Everybody meets the partner that they themselves deserve.

- Do not force or persuade a person to change in a way which they are not yet ready for.

Also take some time to think about the advantage you gain from the behaviour that seemingly bothers you in your partner.

What decision does this behaviour relieve you of? What decision that you do not want to make yet does this behaviour challenge you to take anyway?

What in your own behaviour do you justify by it?

Are you ready to draw strength to act from your honest answers?

Resolving Personal Entanglements

Are you looking for a way to resolve personal entanglements in a loving way? Would you perhaps also like to do something for other people you love?

"A very quick and effective way to your personal solution and truth is "Systemic Family Constellations" by
94

Bert Hellinger". Here, the 'orders of love' are restored completely free of blame.

This way you get a quick overview about general issues in your family or organisation system. This can serve as an aid to decision-making and a basis for changes which you can implement afterwards. It is always interesting to do this and often brings new information to light."

You might already have seen a lot of such and similar kinds of advertisements or flyers on family constellations. What you read about it inspires great hope. I myself have also been somewhat fascinated by this work for many years, but I was always missing something I could not put my finger on. Who would not wish to put their lives in order in a simple way? For me it absolutely did not work. Personally, I could not affect any appreciable change in my life with classic family constellations. Sometimes I had the impression that I was at least getting a certain overview of broad relationship structures that way.

However, my primary interest has always been to visualise unknown structures with burdensome effects and achieve sustainable personal changes on the causal level. For this purpose, classic family constellations have proved to be completely useless for me. As I know now, they also carry some risks which I will describe in more detail.

For me, the essence of classic family constellations can be described in seven words.

He who doesn't honour his parents lives the wrong way!
You will repeatedly encounter this "message" in connection with classic family constellations. For me, this idea is based on an old tradition which is more interested in an obedient mass than a loving society. This is mostly about adaptation to an external form and standard and less about the individual development of autonomy and one's own ability to love. This is especially evident in the effort to transfer the usually illusory "healthy form" into the inner soul image by shifting persons to "standardised" places.

Hint:
For children who have been traumatised by their parents, the "honouring of the parents" in classic family constellations leads to renewed injury of the child. At best, a level of compassion can be created for the negative experiences the parents had had themselves. This can assist in understanding the mechanisms in our society. It is however not appropriate in these cases to honour the parents for suffering inflicted on their own child because by doing so, this suffering child would be betrayed and traumatised all over again! Therefore, never let yourself be forced to honour parents who do not deserve it during any family constellation work! Where humaneness was betrayed and trampled underfoot, it is counterproductive and still dangerous even for the adult child!

My search for more effective ways has led me from family constellation to trauma constellation according to Prof Dr Franz Ruppert. In Part 5 you will find further information on this topic in sections "Karmic Relation-ships" and "TRAUMA".

**Remember that you are worth it to find the space
that suits your requirements for such work!
And where is love in all that?**

**Love
is not something you ask for;
Love
is something people tell each other;
What's even better though
is to feel it
under the skin.**

Misunderstandings, New Ways to Perceive Love and Partnership

Note:
Love is not a cake to be shared in the best possible way, but a state of consciousness which everyone is obliged to expand.

Love does not automatically gain "quality and depth" by being spread among just a few people.

In your conscious being you can only experience those things for which you currently have space in your consciousness. Your feeling of being alive will increase and intensify according to how much you allow yourself to expand your tangible space with love.

This is mainly about awareness and respect for other parts of the creation (humans included!).

Point of Reference:

If love is divided up, it crumbles like dust and ash. If love is expanded, it grows and continues to grow unstoppably until eventually it envelops everything.

Allow me to give you another last bit of advice in order to avoid false interpretations:

My recommendation to expand your feeling of love until there is space for more and more parts of creation is neither an invitation to infidelity (classic cheating) nor a free pass for sexual escapades and the like. The love I am talking about here is a very pleasant, impartial form of free energy without sexual claim. Its source is unlimited, free and is available to everyone without exception. If you feel the need for sexual experiences with other people, you should be very responsible about that, especially if you are in an existing partnership. This calls for great honesty and poses the challenge to explore the true source of desires.

For many people a partnership becomes a kind of perseverance and survival training.

Life is however not about learning to tolerate someone for as long as possible. It is more about opening yourself up to a partner who is able to accept the size and creativity of one's own soul, without feeling personally threatened by it.

If I expect to meet a partner who can "tolerate" me and accept me as I am, I should foster my own ability to let other people be as they are in their natural state, without judging them. Every "yes, but" – "actually" – "why are you like this" and "why are you doing that again", etc. is a mirror of your own unsolved learning tasks. What we perceive as our own inability to love someone else unconditionally only discloses the clear challenge to examine one's own life issues for as long as it takes until all those "yes, but" – "really" etc. have disappeared.

There is a simple rule:

Those who "suffer" most in a relationship still have the biggest insights to come in this regard!

Most people do not really understand the challenge which they have written as a situation into their own play script at some point in order to learn from it, or the role which the necessary supporters play in this context.

This leads to a basic misunderstanding regarding one's partner's role.

If your partner changed in such a way that you would not have to "suffer" anymore, you might finally feel that you really are loved properly. You would however have avoided the learning task which is important for you as well as the actual, self-created challenge.

With each attempt to try and change another person and to apportion "guilt" to them, we try to put our responsibility for changing ourselves on others. However, true love leaves their own learning tasks to the partner and does not take away their chance to grow beyond themselves, to expand their "conceivable r o o m" and to experience the true lightness of being. This is a question of personal life issues and major transformation through knowledge.

Take good care of yourself and do not overburden yourself unnecessarily. If the issue of your life has become clear to you, you should preferably approach your goal rather slowly and gradually. Perhaps you have met a person who gives you the feeling of being accepted as you are, but you yourself have "nothing" to counter that. With your inner willingness to work on yourself and to change your life patterns, you have perhaps attracted clear and strong "mirrors" in your life. But not everyone who is a good mirror for you will be the right life partner for you in the long run. The ease with which you are achieving your own steps of development is a good measure for the "mirror strength" that is best for you in your current phase.

Simply open yourself to a level of partnership which does not always overtax you and does not bring you to your personal limits of consciousness. Allow yourself a spiritual development in playful ease within a framework of boundless wellbeing. Who says that development within a partnership should not be funny or always escalate into stress?

Those who expect
love from others
which they cannot
give to themselves
will always
live with a feeling
of deficiency.

The sun gives its light to the moon without any questions or expectations. In doing so, the sun loses nothing, but the whole world gains from it and loves the sun. The people rejoice at the moonlight, but only very few understand the natural principle of unconditional love which shows itself in it. The topics of relationship, partnership and family are not about learning to divide one's own love, but rather to extend one's own ability to love to infinity. It is important to keep developing this ability, so that more and more people (animals, plants ...) become affected by it and included in it.

We are however not talking about "blind love" here, which covers all "shadows". On the contrary. True love has the power, wisdom and clarity to call the truth by its name. It does not however have to repay "like" with "like".

Note:

People who cannot love themselves, who experience solitude only as loneliness and do not hold their own self in the highest regard, will experience any form of relationship mainly as problematic.

It is especially important in a partnership to show yourself to be as open, honest, vulnerable and wonderful as you are. The goal is not to achieve what the other has in order to be complete!

When two free, self-realised people meet, something develops in the joint connection that is far greater than only the sum of both parts.
With a natural ease and simplicity both enjoy tremendous growth and healing with many joyful experiences. They can find common approaches leading to simple solutions even in difficult circumstances.
Those who give up on themselves in a partnership try to go around the "shadow of the other" and bury the power to realise their own dreams out of misunderstood love. The responsibility for it remains!

Point of Reference:

Each partner mirrors for us how far we have already developed our capacity for personal freedom, autonomy and heart love. Each shadow in our relationship is an indication that the incarnation of our own divinity is not yet complete. With an ideal partner, unexplained shadows of our own karmic history will become visible! And then?

When you stand before a mirror and see hairs hanging down the face – WHO are you combing?

"And what if my partner hits me?"

Then you can have them locked up. Yet if you don't find a clear answer and the reason why you attract a partner who hits you, you must not be surprised if similar things keep happening to you again and again!

It is nothing,
you said in answer
to my asking glance
and barely touched
the ground
with your feet
while doing so.

Really,
you said
and could not hide
the shine
in your eyes.

Believe me,
you asked for it
and I
did it–
should I
have done
anything other
than giving
you my blessing
and the freedom,
the way
you spoke about him
without words,
in love?

22/05/1999

Partnership and Family

One of the biggest challenges for a partnership is the family. Although many people cope with this issue brilliantly, there are also many unanswered questions, apparent contradictions and basic misunderstandings in this particular area. The area with the most uncertainties at the same time also holds the most important learning tasks for all persons involved.

Children have ultrasensitive antennas for adults' inconsistent messages. Therefore, the "quality" of parental care will decide whether a child is experiencing an emotional deficit or not. It is particularly the intensity of undivided attention that is perceived by children as parental love. Physical presence alone is not the kind of presence a child needs to feel safe and loved. It is not about how many hours you spend with your child every day. It is rather about how many minutes a day you can be perceptibly and fully present for a child. With your body, soul and spirit. Where is the presence of a person who is consciously or unconsciously constantly preoccupied with what they lack themselves?

The more parents give up their own visions, goals, desires, friends, hobbies, etc. for their child/children, the more their children get the feeling of being deprived of something in their lives too!

Children can cope much better by themselves than parents often want to admit. Frequently however, children serve parents as an excuse for evading the

responsibility to develop their own visions with courage. Yet such determination on the part of the parents
would be exactly the kind of example that a child
needs so badly. How should a child pluck up the courage later in life to take personal visions seriously?
Where is it supposed to find an example and the
strength to achieve their goals if self-denial apparently
forms part of the survival training?

Have you ever asked yourself who you actually are –
in the eyes of a small child – if you are not yourself?
How can you be yourself, if you give yourself up along
with what is important to you? Do you realise (if this is
really your issue) that the burden of responsibility for
your "burned dreams" will rest on the child's shoulders? No child in the world would accept that
voluntarily. On the contrary. Children need nothing
more urgently than role models for a self-fulfilled life
"despite" family. If you give up your dreams, you lose
yourself, your partner and your children. Then eventually you get into a deep life crisis and once again start
to look for what gives you strength, what lets you be
yourself - your visions! Do you need this detour?

On an emotional level, children uncover the lies of
their parents faster than those lies are spoken.

Rule for Parents

> **The freedoms that parents grant their children should not be greater than the freedoms the parents grant themselves!**

What Could You Learn for Your Relationships From This Part?

I would like you to take away the following from Part 3:

If a part
of your past
lies in the dark,
one day
these shadows
will fall
on your present.

The ideal partner is always one with whom those things become visible and perceptible for you that refer to unexplained shadows in your own life story.

Who is responsible for the fulfilment of your desires?

Santa Claus? Snow White? Hopefully you can guess the good and the bad news. The only person who is really responsible for the fulfilment of your desires is YOURSELF!

You can attract your ideal partner if you realise, understand and resolve what is still just keeping him away from you! Almost any relationship can develop into an ideal partnership, provided both partners are willing to take responsibility for resolving their own issues.

Parents who avoid the shadows of their own dreams and life history are unquestionably responsible for their children growing up in these shadows.

Children who grow up in the shadows of their parents' dreams and life history have the responsibility to move away from these shadows and develop the truth of their own desires, dreams and feelings. It is important to know: For children the taboos and "blind spots" of their parents and previous generations act like magnets, since it is often only there that the strong feelings can be found that are necessary for survival and bonds. If parents had to split off their desires, love and feelings, children can only adhere to their parents' or grandparents' repressed "emotional" stories. That way, children and adults often live in the external emotions and dramas of their grandparents. Other people's feelings thus often become a sad substitute.

Checklist for Part 3 – What Exactly Can You Do Right Now?

Step 3:

Clearing Up of Your Open Desires

Write down spontaneously and honestly what springs to mind when you read the following questions:

- For which life dream have you not developed a plan yet?

- Which life dream have you sacrificed to your relationship, children or job?

- What are the five characteristics your ideal partner absolutely must have?

- Which of the five characteristics expected from your ideal partner do you have yourself?

- What are the five characteristics your ideal partner absolutely must not have?

- Which of the five characteristics your ideal partner must not have do you have yourself?

- What is your biggest fear when you think about a new relationship?

- What do you consider your biggest misfortune, your biggest disappointment?
- What are you missing most in your current relationship?

- What did you miss most in your last relationship?

- Are you able to express feelings of love and admiration spontaneously?

- Is it possible for you to enjoy sexuality with your partner?

- Where have you placed yourself in your relationship, but still are not happy?

Take responsibility for your own open desires, taboo themes and all unresolved feelings associated with them. Handle your issues openly, honestly and mindfully. Whether you are single, in a private or professional relationship – allow yourself to feel the things that still make your life happiness seem incomplete and be very specific in writing them down on a checklist.

For each CURRENT state which is worth improving (feelings, appearance, weight, finances ...), develop a very specific 10-step plan on how to reach your DESIRED state in a realistic way from today's perspective. You can also use the "Plan B for the fulfilment of desires" from Part 2.

The quickest way to achieving change and to finding your ideal partner:

Take any "deficiency" you feel completely and 100% as a desire into your own responsibility. Even if it is difficult – do not let yourself be tempted by others to slide down from this power of responsibility and ability to act to the "waiting bench" defined by dependencies.

The greatest danger to miss your ideal partner:
All thoughts, seconds, and words that you waste on reproaches, accusations or expectations in relation to others get you entangled into a state of victimhood and expectation which is determined by dependence and no longer allows you to be able to act one hundred percent.

Since we grow up as dependent beings, there are always people who are more or less responsible for our CURRENT state. The dissolution from the entanglements of such relationships which might well be necessary is also our own responsibility.

The steps you need to take are part of this guide. This part is especially about your desires, goals and your "Plan B for the fulfilment of your partnership needs".

Your parents may carry a lot of responsibility for your "CURRENT state".

They are however not responsible at all for your choosing not to leave the "hammock" of this state and for your only creativity consisting of the formulation of new blame, accusations and demands. More constructive ways are described in the following chapters.

At this point I would like to make you especially aware that you can only reach your partnership "WISH state" if you take complete 100% responsibility for it. You already know how it feels when other people take responsibility for your "CURRENT state".
In other words:

Do not put your future in the hands of persons who are responsible for a present you do not like!

Clarify your past as necessary. But keep the perpetrators from your past out of the plans for your future! You alone are responsible for your ideal partner.

If your partnership "WISH state" does not intensely motivate you to do your "homework", your "wish list" is either as inspiring and erotic as a mole hill or you are still living in massive perpetrator symbioses, trauma structures or illusions about yourself.

Now let us take a closer look at the karmic aspects concerning the topic of partnerships.

Karmic Relationships

Karmic relationships
are often
like the encounter
of two ticking time bombs.

Separation
is often
a form of divine assistance
to prevent worse from happening
if "disarming the bomb"
has not succeeded in time.

Use the space
to finally
look deeper.

Release your soul
from this drama
and remove the explosives
from your life
and your karmic path
with divine help.

Part 4: The Secret of Karmic Relationships

Most p e o p l e
have nothing but demands,
and what's more,
demands on other people.

Partnerships and the Secrets of Karmic Relationships

The human being in the maelstrom of effects

Most humans live in a maelstrom of effects without recognising the true causes of the consequences they experience.

We always experience the principle of cause and effect as personal Karma.

When we meet other people, we experience a mixture of different levels which due to our ignorance often leads to misunderstandings and conflicts. Especially in closer contact with other people we encounter the central themes of life such as guilt, responsibility and love as well as their projections. When people meet, their various karmic structures mix, often leading to situations (new, self-created Karma) which we cannot classify. That's why we often carry conflicts with us which suddenly even seem to increase in a partnership with another person – for no apparent reason.

**With the right people
many questions
do not arise
or
even more so than ever**.

16/05/1999

In order to understand the topic of partnership, it is necessary to consider the basic principles and sense of the forces working in them.

In order to get closer to the meaning of partnership in the karmic sense, I would like to take a closer look at the components involved, one by one and independently of each other.

General Information on Partnership

A partnership is a form of interpersonal community which combines certain common goals and interests. Partnerships can be found on many levels in life – with very different degrees of personal involvement.

A partner can be an associate, comrade, playfellow, opponent or a friend. Therefore, a partnership can assume a business, social or private form. Partnership is the term for any form of relationship between at least two people. Most people associate a partnership with living together in an interpersonal relationship. The level or depth of such a relationship is determined solely by those who enter into such a connection. Partnership can also take on an exterior form which is

118

visible to other people. For example, there are business partnerships (limited partnerships) in business or marriage in the private area. In the social area we encounter, for example, table tennis partners and countless other types of partnerships. The duration of a partnership may be limited to a particular time-span – for the duration of a game – but usually this is not the case. The term "partnership" is normally used to refer to a more permanent connection between people.

Partnership usually includes practicing together, learning from and with each other and exchanging views and experiences in order to enhance one's personal skills and knowledge with the aim to achieve individual and / or common goals.

Through partnership, many people want to reach some kind of mastery. The intensity of the joint training will determine the possible degree of success. The expansion of the individual personality is the necessary foundation to achieve common goals.

A chess club, for example, will only become a winner on points in the tournament if as many individual players as possible can win their respective points games. This provides motivation for the individual players to improve their own skills, but also to support and promote their chess partners at their own club. This basic principle can be found at all levels and in all forms of partnerships.

Partnership is based on mutual support and the implementation of impulses which are brought into the union as contributions from both parties.

The German word component "... –schaft" in "Partner-schaft", meaning partnership is, though this is not well known, an independent term from mechanics. "Schaft" is the smooth cylindrical part of a screw between the screw head and the thread, in English called the shank. The shank has a stabilising and – in the direction of the thread – power transmitting function. Often this part is slightly conical, that is, tapered in the direction of the thread, slightly "pointed". The screw itself is used to <u>establish a reversible connection</u> or to transfer a rotational movement into a longitudinal one.

In screw propellers for example, the rotational movement is converted into <u>thrust</u>.

Therefore, a partnership also involves the transmission and conversion of energies which are brought into the partnership by the partners themselves or by others.

Whether the partnership manages to implement and stabilise the intensity of such released impulses depends on the willingness of the partners to accept the impulses.

If the partners succeed in converting these energies and steer them in a particular direction, they will strengthen their partnership together and at the same time trigger a thrust which will propel them powerfully towards their goal. Partnership in its basic meaning therefore points towards a connection between people who are confronted with active and dynamic forces that need to be transformed. Partnership also always means individual development as well as at least one common goal.

If this context cannot be understood, partnership cannot exist, be lived or accomplished in the sense of the original meaning.

With this in mind it will now become interesting to look at the karmic aspect of partnership. To that end it is important to first of all explain the basic concept of "Karma".

**Love
is like a dream
we often
close ourselves to
because we fear
we might wake up
one day.**

08/04/1999

K a r m a

"Karma" is the central term in Buddhism. Translated from Sanskrit, "Karma" means something like "consequence" or "effect".

We also know the law of Karma – the law of cause (plan) + effect.

To ease you into the topic I have provided you with a link to a short video about the cause and effect principle. Here, "Karma" is explained in a unique way in just 2 minutes and 37 seconds.

www.karmische-beziehung.de/karma

Please understand that this offer is only available for as long as the holder of the license rights allows its use. – Have fun

Karma is always the result of a human being manipulating something through their ego.

The past of a human being (also from other lives) creates his present. What a human being does now – creates his future. Therefore, Karma also means "doing".

KARMA

Barely
arrived,
people
judge
others.

31/05/1993

But not every cause (deed) has an inevitable effect – it is always possible to create a timely balance. The future can always be influenced to 100%. Karma wants to convey that you always bear personal responsibility for everything what happens. The law of Karma demands that you accept personal responsibility and do not project any guilt on others. Karma also explains through the laws of cause + effect that there is no such thing as coincidence.

Everyone goes through all those particular problems which they avoided in the past and have therefore not yet consciously accepted and integrated.

Karma as an energy body

You can imagine Karma as an energy body, in which certain, unresolved human experiences are stored. You have to neutralise and delete these experiences until all Karma is resolved when you finally reach your goal. With the dissolution of Karma, another incarnation becomes unnecessary, at least on the planet Earth. Remark: in carnere = to become flesh (word stem).

This kind of storage in the energy body is not bound by time or space.

Karmic

"Karmic" in this context means the repetition of certain experiences as a learning process, until unclarified themes from the past are accepted and processed.
A person's ability to make their own free decision on the H o w and W h e r e does not get lost this way.

Dissolution of Karma

Especially in the interpersonal field, Karma is a natural balancing system of non-harmonised energies of the past. That's why some people keep meeting again d again under the same or similar circumstances, until both understand their personal part in it and implement the knowledge from it for their future existence.

The principle of repetition of some problems confronts us with the personal parts of our ego which are the true bridge to enlightenment for us. That's the reason this learning process through repetition (law of rhythm) is especially valuable to us. However, something can only repeat until I recognise what it is. When I wake up, understand and reconsider, I dissolve Karma and leave the cycle of repetition of a particular topic which has hitherto been necessary. This cycle of repetition meets us at all levels of our lives. Since people are forgetful and lazy, they usually do not think about such mechanisms.

Partnership as a Karmic Key

No matter on which level, our partner always holds a special position. As a result, we generally have a greater willingness to consider emerging problems and conflicts. This willingness opens our consciousness to a discussion about issues that in a karmic sense mean the key to transformation for us.

For us, this is a way we can balance out the consequences of causes that were set previously. The more consciously this process happens, the sooner we learn to live in the "now", in absolute self-honesty, and to take complete responsibility for everything we do.

This is the basis for a future partnership in loose affinity. In order for Karma to still have meaning for a partnership in this clarified future, we need new impulses that trigger further, also partnership-orientated development processes on other levels.

Karmic partnership I

In a Karmic sense, partnership is a special opportunity for us to restore harmony wherever we have hurt others with our ego.

Karmic partnership II
Karma as the soul's shadow

Therefore, from karmic point of view, any form of partnership for me has mainly to do with the soul's shadow. The aim is to recognise, understand and release one's own shadows with the partner's help and support. This happens through the mirror effect which the partner unconsciously activates in their capacity as an aid to fulfilment.

**The more I
became the way
who you always wished me to be,
the more
I confronted
you with
what you have been
afraid of for so long –
to lose
a beloved person
again.**

Through the transformation of Karma, a light-consciousness develops that increasingly rids the soul of its shadows. When the soul dissolves into light, the cycle of Karma is broken.

In terms of its karmic properties, partnership also means a great challenge to me and is a unique opportunity to accelerate processes of personal development. Moreover, partnership also offers the challenge and opportunity to develop characteristics such as humility, love, care and gratitude.

The more consciously the "shadow work" in the partnership was resolved karmically, the stronger the energy of light flows into the partnership. Therefore, karmically a partnership for me also means a possible way to the light.

Karmic Partnership

Karmic partnerships carry a particularly great learning potential.

They stand out by a particularly intense exchange of forces within the partnership. Unresolved experiences of earlier pasts usually assume a destructive form and connect the partners with a seemingly inexplicable love-hate relationship.

This form of partnership desperately needs spiritual content in order to survive and to be understood.

You will learn more about the secrets of karmic relationships shortly.

Your smile shines
in my heart,
with a single glance
your big eyes
open
my soul,
Your closeness
touches me
warmly
and deeply –
the wheel of life
watches on with respect,
but it cannot stop
time
anymore.

What is a Karmic Relationship?

In order to understand the importance of a karmic relationship, it is helpful to first of all comprehend the term **KARMA** in all its magnitude. As already mentioned, it is the key term in Buddhism. It describes a cycle of cause and effect as a consequence of our conscious or unconscious will.

Karma results from personal actions (deeds), words and thoughts, the "seeds" of which continue to influence timelessly. Karma is therefore often described as the timeless sum of personal actions. Karma remains beyond time and space and many incarnations (this and other lives, soul journey / soul travelling / rebirths). You do not have to subscribe to this idea in order to make use of its principles! Even in this one life, the timeless laws of cause + effect are at work.

Any action or inaction can create or change Karma.

Karma can be changed, converted, dissolved, transformed and accumulated.

The term "karmic" refers either to the fact that situations experienced in the "Now" are affected by influences and events which have already taken place or that the events which are just taking place have an effect beyond the current situation.

> **Note:**
> **Our personal actions can at any point launch a new cycle of cause and effect which leads to new karmic connections! Karma is always the sum of our timeless history up to now.**

How Do Karmic Relationships and Karmic Connections Develop?

A karmic relationship develops as soon as we include another being (human, animal, plant, planet ...) in one of our actions, the effect of which is not karmically neutral. Our personal intention (karmic will) is of greater importance than the achieved result. Even a failure to act may produce a karmic relationship to all beings that might be affected by it. An accident in winter as a consequence of a failure to change to winter tyres, for example, creates a karmic obligation to compensate and to help any "accident victims" who might have been injured in the process. Any failure to lend assistance (if a real need is present), failure to carry out a safety inspection or the like can result in karmically effective events and create new connections that have the characteristic of a karmic relationship. The relationship Karma in this relationship can be very positively supportive, negatively burdensome or a wild mixture of both. The type and quality of a karmic rela-

130

tionship reflect the quality of the common "seed" from the past. In connections which are difficult today it thus reveals the chance to resolve burdensome karmic patterns.

What Does the Term "Karmic Relationship" Actually Mean?

The term "karmic relationship" points to a connection between two souls who know each other very well, perhaps because they have already met in previous lives. On an interpersonal level, the term simply means that at least one act by one or more persons led to a karmic bond between at least two people / souls through which the people involved are still in a relationship today.

This act might be something that happened in this or any previous lives. **Any connection, even one creat-**

ed mentally, leads to a timeless, karmically effective relationship.

The term "karmic relationship" naturally also includes karmic connections on a partnership level; that's what it related to it originally but it is not limited to it! Literature often neglects this universal aspect of karmic relationships and thereby often makes it difficult for the inexperienced observer to gain access to the real crux of the issue. It thus blocks the spiritual view of beneficial pathways. See also "Karmic Relationship and Regression".

A problematic karmic relationship frequently cannot be changed by one person alone within the relationship. However, the originally binding, onerous karmic element and pattern may well be unilaterally dissolved completely and continue to work positively beyond the relationship.

In case of separations (business, private, partnership, family), some people later get the opportunity to meet each other again. If, in the meantime, the successful transformation (complete conversion / resolution) of karmic patterns has been achieved, those people will realise that the earlier, burdensome karmic patterns were the only binding or separating elements!

A joint honest look at what there really is "now" can lead to profound healing in a new encounter. The conscious experience of karmic influences and the experience of liberated encounters within one's own karmic journey can be a considerable, touching gift and lead to formative insights into the "laws of Karma".

> **Note:**
> The only binding or separating element in a
> "karmic" relationship is often a burdensome
> "karmic" pre-history!

Karmic Relationship and Regression

Particularly karmic relationships of any kind can be subject to rapid and profound change by clarification of burdensome influences which are no longer obvious. If you consider the possibility of several incarnations (soul journeys), it is a great challenge for many souls to clarify the confusion which arises from different kinds of encounters – husband-wife, daughter-father, mother-son, brother-sister, woman-woman, man-man, boss-employee.... – during multiple lifetimes. When working through them, it is therefore important to decipher the deeper reason for a karmic relationship, independent of the changes in role relationships during the karmic journey. If you are ready to clear up the real reason for a burdensome karmic relationship, regression can also provide helpful information on the origins of the karmic relationship. The method of reincarnation therapy does involve the risk of escape projections to other worlds or lives though, which even many therapists fall for again and again. Since many people conduct regression work in rather an unprofessional manner only and miss important steps, I would like to recommend, in my capacity as a reincarnation therapist, that you start with the resolution of entanglements and the clearing up of burdensome effects in the present life. That way you can make sure that a therapist doesn't misguide you into shifting the clarification of problems from your present or childhood into a previous life.

Meanwhile, I also prefer using "intention" according to Prof Dr Franz Ruppert for my work in clearing up karmic relationships. You will find out more about that later. This method widens the possibilities with regards to regression very clearly and also establishes the necessary connection between cause and effect in your life for you, directly and comprehensibly. Questions and alleged facts can be checked relatively promptly this way.

With my knowledge and practical experience of multi-generational psycho-traumatology as a reincarnation therapist, I come to the conclusion that information on "previous lives" largely also points to entanglements with "other lives", i.e. other persons. The entanglement with the lives of others is made transparent by the phenomenon of symbiosis / trauma and bonding system trauma. A lot of the information that comes up during regression belongs to the multigenerational family system with which we as descendants had to bond emotionally during the phase of early childhood dependency.

Since we cannot distinguish between our own and foreign feelings during the phase of early childhood, we start to absorb the energetic and emotional heritage of our family through symbiosis from as early as the moment of our conception. In the womb, we are literally swamped with impressions as well as alien feelings and "histories".

Everything is included there: from unhappy love to lost children, expelled or murdered family members, accidents, secret liaisons, unknown siblings, violence, mental distress, escape, persecution or betrayal. Many lives = many stories.

This way, deep bonds and feelings can form to people we have never seen before.
So if your head is swirling with innumerable images, dreams and stories, you now know why.

From today's perspective I would therefore suggest that you clear up the burdensome symbioses with your own family system first, before you start reincarnation therapy. By doing so, you will quickly develop a feeling for your own feelings and your own life story. If any inexplicable phenomena are still left after that, regression therapy can provide helpful information and new ideas for further clarification. In most cases this will not be necessary though.
Now the possibility of a new relationship perspective is in your hands.

Karmic Relationship and Love – Couple Relationships

We often talk about a karmic relationship in the context of an imperfect, unhappy love. On a partnership level, karmic relationships are often characterised by passionate, intense feelings of all kinds. If love from the heart is not free there, the "passion" as the karmic mirror shows the original chance, shape and dimension of the timeless bond that still causes suffering today. In these cases in particular, the deep ignorance of the issue of karmic entanglements leads to many dramatic experiences. Those who look deeper, discover precious pearls of knowledge and solid ways to a new karmic freedom in relationships.

> ## Note:
> **The only actual burden in a love relationship is often an old "karmic" pattern!**

Karmic Relationships and "Forbidden", Unfree Love

Here, "forbidden" is defined by the social and legal regulations at the time of the experience. Personal moral convictions are another factor.

The "forbidden" love relationship within the family might be most likely to disclose its karmic origin to the inexperienced observer.

Common forms of "forbidden" love:

- Sibling love with partnership desires and requirements (abuse, deep love – in repression, escape + hate)

- Sexual relationships between parents and children (abuse + deep love)

- Homosexual love

- Another person's partner

- Love between rich and poor

- Love with different maturity – "young + old"

- Different cultures and skin colours

If partner feelings within the family become so strong that waiting for the sexual maturity of the other appears to be impossible, abuse often becomes an outlet and thereby a new mirror of an unfree love. Despite karmic aspects, sexual relationships in the family usually have their origins in unresolved traumas of parents who have experienced sexual abuse themselves.

But there are karmic love relationships which result in a confusing parent-child, sibling or similarly difficult form of relationship. Here the timeless desire of two souls to be finally reunited becomes visible. This is based on the karmic pattern of an old promise to prove love and loyalty for ever and ever, across all boundaries. Against all resistance by others, an oath was sworn in the past, showing what even "then" was already an unfree love.

Out of ignorance, helplessness and despair, this unfree love was often sealed in a magical, ritualistic way and therefore persists to this day in its unfree unredeemed form! Often such love was additionally covered with negative energy structures of all kinds (curse, spell, etc.) by envious people and enemies to ensure its failure.

If you allow yourself to feel deep inside what this means for you, you might understand why I recommend to you at this point to completely release your ex-partner. According to my experience it is not possible to dissolve the unhappy form of love without letting the partner go.

It is important in these cases to clear and heal the origin of this love which was unfree even back then. The complete resolution of unhappy energy structures can only be checked in full and mutual freedom.

A "forbidden love" can often be accompanied by desire and dream memories of sexual encounters in past lives. Out of fear to admit and experience a "forbidden" love, it is repressed so strongly for self-protection on both sides that it turns into self-loathing and hatred or sometimes even ends in an act of destruction.

It happens that siblings develop such a deep love for each other that it also calls for a physical encounter and relationship. Due to social and legal prohibitions, this desire is usually suppressed and remains unspoken. It is not only between siblings who seemingly don't have anything to say to each other that on closer examination you will find a protective wall of fear and avoidance to tell each other "the one thing". Because this is about deep emotional entanglements and injuries of the soul, no one can resolve the problem rationally. Healing is reserved for those who are willing to once more immerse themselves briefly in the main traumatic events, as if in fast forward mode, and to experience these feelings from a new perspective. By rediscovering of the whole karmic history of a relationship, it is possible to redeem it deliberately. The pain which has accompanied those concerned for many years becomes a source of joy and strength when transformed. That way, siblings can find a new level of being together again in free love, without the inner compulsion to also experience it in form of a physical love relationship.

Point of Reference:
Those who have nothing to say to each other are often simply avoiding saying "the one thing". Some people distance themselves so far (emotionally / physically) that they cannot get too close to the beloved other person! Thus, separation sometimes becomes an escape from the danger of becoming the perpetrator through abuse of a beloved person.

Note:
Unfree love was often sealed magically and ritually and therefore persists to this day in its unfree, unredeemed form.

Karmic Patterns in Relationship, Love and Partnership

I would like to give you a particular example:

A formative event: In a former life the wife in a couple became the victim of a violent crime on her wedding day. She dies before the official ceremony. During regression, a young soul appeared next to her – a new life of which she did not know. The emotional drama imprints a timeless trauma in both souls of the partnership – loss, pain, confusion, helplessness in the particular real event. At the same time, a timeless karmic relationship pattern develops - <u>marriage</u> is dangerous, it results in a drama, has a traumatic end, <u>it must be avoided at all costs.</u>

From this experience, a karmic relationship pattern develops:
New encounters in later life offer many opportunities and wonderful experiences. Everything is possible, except for one thing: a wedding! When it comes to marriage, alarm bells sound for at least one of partners. Even invitations from friends to their weddings trigger strange feelings. Participation in other weddings inevitably causes great distress. The mind says, "You are crazy", "Stay calm", "You are only imagining all that"; but one of them remembers: "Marriage is dangerous" ... The heart is scared a n d is right – the karmic time bomb is already ticking again! How much time do you have?

Hint:
Therefore, do not force your partner if you do not want to risk being left standing at the wedding altar. Take vague fears and feelings seriously. The information about a "previous life" can also refer to an event in the family history which still has an unclarified entanglement attached to it. I consciously refrain from a therapeutic analysis of all possible backgrounds here. You won't find it at all difficult to transfer this example to a chain of events which takes place within any life – a woman loses her husband on their wedding day, wants to marry again ten years later but from the moment she makes that decision she increasingly starts to have "panic attacks" ...

But let me continue with the example which includes the possibility of various incarnations.

Encounter in this life:
Our pair of souls meets again in this life as man and woman in the course of their further development. An age difference is insignificant, social or cultural gaps are also not in the way. Both have been interested in spiritual issues and personal development for some time and would probably never have run into each other in normal life. Thus, a spontaneous private date in surprising intimacy and harmony results in an uncomplicated, sensually erotic partnership. They help each other to grow and to heal old wounds. Anything is possible but "to speak of love would be a lie". A very deep "liking" brings the two people together with great ease and naturalness. Since qualities such as mindfulness, tolerance and appreciation are already well developed in their personality, they talk openly about

the fact that they do not feel the great heart love for each other despite all the beauty. Working on this theme could not change that either. Attempts to give each other freedom again in order to find the genuine love somewhere else also fail miserably. After a time of separation they come together again as if nothing had happened. This goes on for several years, until the widowed mother of the woman dies, which launches another karmic maelstrom in which the man is unconsciously involved.

The desire to talk openly to his partner about love became stronger and stronger due to the sorrowful circumstances of the death. When one day the man put the fulfilment of his heart's desires into divine hands, fate took its course. At a seminar about deep transformation and release of karma, he met another woman with whom he felt spontaneously joined in deep and genuine love. Since this feeling could not be transferred to the existing partnership and the man wanted to live in his love without secrets, a painful separation followed which also threw the man into the greatest crisis of his life. He had to leave the feel-good relationship and the dream woman he'd been with over many lives in order to follow the "divine" order and to discover the secret of the genuine love. In doing so, he felt deserted, cut off from life and somehow stranded in no man's land. It happened to him and the two women and no one could seriously have prevented it.

He was now in contact with his genuine love and still as far away from life and happiness as never – other relationships can never fill the gap of a failed, unfortunate karmic relationship before its origins are "healed"!

The man discovered himself on an inner karmic journey as an unwanted lost male child by the side of his abandoned partner's buried mother. Thus, his partner lost her "brother" for the second time in a lifetime, without knowing or understanding it. And the man thus lost his partner and "sister", although this knowledge could not really ease his sorrow. The karmic wheel simply keeps turning and only those who look deeper understand the trace of the soul. In this case, it was found that the buried mother of his abandoned partner had lost another female child before it could incarnate. With the genuine love the man had found this "other sister" again as well as the challenge of embracing complete transformation. With each of these puzzle pieces the soul became somewhat calmer, the view clearer.

In the work-up and some regression work on the karmic relationship with the former partner, the karmic pattern of a deep love in many forms came to light which repeatedly came to an abrupt, unhappy ending after the lovers had confessed their love to each other and wanted to get married.
In order to protect each other and nevertheless be together, they agreed not to talk about love in further lives. Since an avoidance attitude never leads to salvation, the result was an unhappy and abrupt separation in this life as well.

Our true nature can never be denied permanently. The divine essence within us always strives towards unconditional love.

We are therefore left with the challenge to dissolve the pattern of an unfree karmic love relationship in the origin of its un-freedom. This is often only possible if we are willing to let the other partner go completely into his divine freedom, without any expectation of any new free relationship with him in this or future lives.

Every expectation establishes a new unknown bond which is incompatible with this path of initiation into unconditional love.

Take your chance while your karmic time bomb is still ticking!

A wider view of your own karmic journey can help you step through the gate of life again and to remember self-imposed tasks. Healing and transformation of an unhappy love is possible without separation if both partners call on appropriate help in time and remove any existing "explosives". With this basic knowledge you will gain not only new and important findings in a single session, but you will also be able to fundamentally change relationship structures.

Trust your instincts. On the web you can find a variety of offers.

**Defuse the time bomb
in your life
while it is
still ticking.**

01/03/2007

28 Distinguishing Factors of a Karmic Love Relationship

- Spontaneous encounter or slow mutual discovery in great familiarity.

- A very natural feeling in being together.

- Sensual and erotic encounter, but "to speak of love would be a lie".

- Feel-good relationship, but the genuine love for each other is not free.

- Strong harmony, but somehow it does not feel right to say: I love you!

- Speechlessness and inability to speak.

- Great sympathy, affection and deep love that seems to be inappropriate.

- Joint attempts to free this love fail just like the relationship itself.

- Emotional turmoil and helplessness in the encounter.

- Socially "forbidden" love.

- Combination of the greatest happiness and the greatest suffering.

- Despite great attraction and a deep love, somehow one cannot commit to it and suffers.

- Separations and still never being apart – Time does not heal any wounds.

- Longing, love-hatred, confusion, unanswered questions and conflicting emotions.

- Strong bond in deep pain even many years later.

- This familiar feeling cannot be found in any new, different relationship.

- You feel cheated in love and feel yourself a cheat in love – a constant feeling of only ever reaching second place in a relationship.

- Really, life could be so beautiful – what has actually happened?

- Pulling out at the "last minute" – "leaving as a precaution", to abandon the partner on the wedding day ...

- The separation has deeply hurt you – despite all the despair it was right for you to go.

- The one who leaves the other also feels abandoned – and as a rule they suffer several times over.

- In general, separation stops the karmic pattern but not the confusion or longing.

- The severity of separation / drama of the relationship today cannot be explained by visible events.

- You feel confronted with an "equation with 7 unknowns".

- There is no way in sight to a happy ending.

- The longing and desire to find a healthy way after all, remain for the rest of life.

- Against all obstacles that appear and uninfluenced by other relationships, there is often a secret, inner promise never to leave the other or to give up searching for a solution.

- The one who has "extinguished the fuse" (separates out of fear / courage), can learn to forgive themselves and to completely take apart the "karmic time fuse" in order to dispose of it forever – if they can survive the other's hatred, the mental stoning, their own re-traumatisation and other things.

Note:
Other relationships can never fill the void left by a failed unhappy karmic relationship before it is healed and understood in its origin!

The Real Secret of Karmic Relation- ships – Summary of Karmic Aspects

Each karmic relationship has its origin in an unfree, "forbidden" love. The attraction between the souls remains over many lifetimes. Again and again, they are allowed to encounter each other on their karmic travels in order to release the sorrowful and suppressed feelings. Since this love has never been free, a present new encounter cannot be free either. For that, a full transformation and healing of this issue on both sides is necessary.

Among the trials these souls have to experience on their soul-journey are repeated sudden separations through illness, accidental death, war, violent crime and other events. That's why an unfree "forbidden" love is often characterised by shocks, feelings of guilt and traumatic events. I have encountered this again and again in regression therapy. This is why one day the souls are not free to talk about love anymore. The fear of it being "forbidden" and of misfortune has grown too strong over countless years. In this pain and in unexplained sadness some souls search for ways to finally release their genuine love again in order to burst the constraints of "I like you". This leads to separations and solitary years of searching in despair which no one really understands.

This challenge often cannot be led into the divine order in a "normal way" by the person concerned. Too often these attempts at clearing fail because the entanglements are too vast and spiritual dimensions are not adequately recognised or taken into account. In its desperation and deep concern, every soul searches for a path to redeem this deep pain. Sometimes new ways are tried out together that promise quick relief. This often ends in rituals and forms of magic that bring even greater suffering to that love. The "everlasting effects" of the real issue remain hidden and unclear. The result are numerous painful experiences and incarnations in a cycle that doesn't ever seem to want to end. Yet just a clear new decision before "God / the Divine": "I want to get out of there" may lead to resolution and healing here. This path is rarely short, but it is the only one that leads to a profound, permanent cure and unconditional love in the long term.

In my experience, an important step along this way can be to make a new decision in form of a **"revocation of Black Magic"***. Only you can open the way to a divine solution in this life.

*For a guide see "Orientation Aids and Exercises"
Such a connection can only achieve healing when both partners find out for themselves what the reason was that led them to this unhappy love in the first place. This should happen without judgement or accusations, out of the deep desire to end this suffering forever.

> ## Note:
> **Each partner can take the path to karmic freedom independently of the other and, with appropriate help, clear his karmic mine field bit by bit.**

If even "the enlightened" and so called masters we meet cannot lead us deeper into clearing, the time has come to take our own "master exam".

This information has already changed your consciousness and opened new ways to a self-liberated life. Take this opportunity to open new perspectives on life. Enrich your life with new lightness and joy.

It will be my pleasure to help you untie your karmic knot.

Challenge, Chance and Dissolution of a Karmic Love Relationship

The karmic relationship often leads a person into the deepest suffering, but at the same time it also opens up the chance to grow beyond it. The solution to such a challenge is only possible for people who are willing to be uncomfortable to the point of it being unbearable.

The path leads through the deepest pain and the shadows of the soul to the very basis of guilt and forgiveness. The darkest root of all relationships must be found and healed in order that – blessed in the Divine – a relationship without suffering becomes possible again. Even the "most sacred" of our relationships needs to be granted the karmic freedom of an innocent bond in the face of the Divine. Letting go out of understanding, in deep love, leads even karmic relationships to a healing source in the light of divine grace. If you are willing to take responsibility for all the dark shadows of your soul and to put your heart into divine hands, you do have a chance. Take advantage of the help offered by those who are placed by your side so that you are always aware of the light, even during the darkest years of your journey.

Take the first step, but do not expect someone particular to follow you. Sometimes others only recognise the possible freedom after you have hoisted the flag on your mountain. Therefore, if possible, leave signs along your journey. Some paths are very narrow …

Poems on Karmic Relationships

- **Karmic relationship** (see Part 4 at the beginning)

- **Innocence**

- **Clouds of shadow**

- **Without you**

INNOCENCE

It is not your fault
that I wanted
to tear down the wall
between our hearts
and have followed the love
which was revealed to me
after many prayers.
It is not your fault
that the shadows have been so deep
and the years so dark
since then.

You can easily lose yourself
on the way to the answers
and you seldom meet fellows
like you –
You should know
that you are a great deal
to do with the fact,
that I never give up.

There have been gaps
in the wall,
since that day
when I discovered
our love again
at a scary place.

The pain of separation
in this life
should be the last one
between us though –

there is still light
beyond the shadows.

The stakes
are as high as never before,
but this time
even the longing
is willing to pay
the highest price,
even
if not even you
understand it.

It is not your fault
that I still
love you.

20/11/2007

Clouds of Shadows

If you knew
how much
I miss you,
if you
only suspected
how difficult
it is
to walk this path,
if you
could feel
just for a moment
how I am doing
with all that,
then you might
understand
that all of your dark thoughts
towards me
only make it
more difficult
and improbable
that we ever meet anew
as really free beings
in deep love.

09/02/2008

Without You

Surviving
only this one day
without you –
there is no tomorrow yet.
To breath,
to walk,
to stand
without you
in this moment –
to see
what is left
of me
without you.
Only this particular day
in the third year
is
still difficult now –
there is no
tomorrow yet.

You can find more poems on karmic relationships
at: www.besuca.com

Damals, als Deine Mutter starb | Back then, when your
mother died
Damals und heute | Back then and today
Preis | Price   -   Prüfung | Test
Engel weinen nicht | Angels do not cry* – see also the
end of Part 7

What Could You Learn for Your Relationships from This Part?

From Part 4 I would like you to take away the following:

As soon as you get into a relationship, it is "karmic" – since it is determined by the timeless teachings and cause and effect principles from the beginning.

This refers to any kind of relationship, community or interest group. You yourself determine the quality of your relationship karma.

Experiences in your past relationships characterise your abilities to deal with a relationship, community or interest group today.

The "shadows" of all your karmic relationships determine the realisation of your options, personal desires, goals and dreams.

Experiences can be changed if the deeper context and meaning are understood.

In terms of this guide, a karmic relationship is not necessarily connected to a spiritual way of life or "esoteric" view.

Checklist for Part 4 – What Exactly Can You Do Right Now?

Step 4:

Clearing Up of Your Karmic Pattern

Relationships are often determined by life patterns that we sometimes even recognise as such recurring patterns, but seemingly cannot change.

Let us please take a look at these relationship patterns of yours. Compile a list of all the points, situations, events and behaviour patterns that you have already noticed in the context of your relationships. For this purpose write down especially the reactions and behavioural patterns which you have already noticed in yourself with regards to relationships and found unwanted, unpleasant, embarrassing, inappropriate etc.

What kinds of patterns emerge in relation to separations?
The goal is not to review the individual points, but to create a kind of inventory for better orientation. You can also use the list of characterising factors as a help. I hope that I have already been able to help you to sharpen your awareness of important factors with the information I've given you so far. Now write down the aspects which are applicable for you. The examples are intended as guidance and help.

Situation / Event / Topic – My Action-/ Relationship Pattern

- The topic "children / marriage" – I avoid it, I feel uncomfortable, I change the topic or run away.

- Relationship – No Relationship lasts longer than three years.

- Whenever I want to get married – ... a short time later my partner dies.

- Whenever I fall in love – ... my nightmares start.

- If somebody shows me their love – ... I break off the relationship.

- ...

The recognition and acceptance of "critical" aspects is always the first step. Yes, that is the way it is today. I allow myself to call even uncomfortable relationship patterns specifically by their name. In this sincerity I am authentic. That way I open myself to understanding new possibilities, to finding out what causes and backgrounds my relationship patterns might have.

In this responsibility and in the willingness to understand, changes are possible for me as well.

Recognition, Interpretation and Change of Karmic Relationships in Everyday Life

| **Note:** |
| A karmic relationship is always preceded by an invitation. This invitation is directed at a single person, group or nation. |

You probably know the situation when in the street, in a restaurant or at a party someone starts to insult people loudly, to offend guests or to be intrusive. Perhaps the person just breaks into a very loud monologue or begins to tell a story like a solo entertainer. Now, if you remember a similar situation, you know what I mean. Even if you were not addressed directly, you did probably sense that something was "floating" in the air, something that demanded a response from you. Listen, stop listening, look or look away, stop, go on, find a safe distance but continue to observe what happens, call someone on the phone to distract yourself from it or to let someone know all about it.

In any case, your attention is captured for a short time and this alone shows that the "invitation" has reached you. A similar situation arises when an interesting person glances at you with interest. This first moment is especially important.

In scientific terms, each invitation is the basis for a new equation with a hitherto unknown result. Since the invitation has reached you and captured your attraction, you became a part of the equation although you perhaps did not even want that. In a karmic sense, nothing has happened yet. Since there hasn't been any reaction on your part (effect / action), the invitation just floats in the air. The equation looks like this: cause + effect = relationship karma; invitation + (your reaction = 0) = invitation.

Very often, the first moment of a cause is neutral! Like an advertisement in your letter box.

You now decide – often in seconds – what you are going to do with it. It is your reaction that now decides whether and how you enter into a relationship with the other person or an event. Your deed is the actual essential key, not always the invitation or cause.

Your reaction to something or someone, your deed, your action alone is the deciding factor in what is going to happen next. Especially in interpersonal relationships we often forget this essential point and therefore always follow the same reaction patterns. Some of these patterns are ones we have unconsciously copied from our parents or grandparents, others were shaped by our resistance against the family. Of course, there are reasons for this as well. In order to help you understand many of these reasons, I wrote *The Secret of Karmic Relationships*. Do you know the saying, "Imagine that there is a war and nobody turns up for battle"? Always check carefully whose "war" you are fighting!

My advice for your everyday life: For immediate implementation and application:

Attach a mental sign saying "invitation" to any person or issue that demands your attention and each event to which you feel invited, willingly or not. Then take two or three relaxed breaths and think about one to three of your most important life goals. Then ask yourself whether and how this invitation is or can be conducive to reaching them. Take another two to three breaths and calmly consider how you are going to react to this invitation according to your current options. The more often you do this, the faster you develop a response pattern that will also help you to act purposefully and according to your needs, even if you have to react immediately and spontaneously.

One of my goals is for example: "a sensual and erotic partnership in unconditional genuine love". How does a car driver fit in here who is cutting me off or fails to give way to me? At first glance this encounter makes no sense. I therefore let him drive on and wish him a pleasant journey. Why am I doing that?

For me, this reaction pattern has the following advantages:

- I do not invest my attention, time and life energy into a new relationship which invites me with a quality I do not wish to share.

- I do not get entangled into the story of a person who seems to be travelling across borders.

- I can take my time to think about who or what the situation reminds me of.

- Before I get entangled with strangers again, I would rather use the chance to discover which persons already known to me I am still connected to by unclarified, cross-border experiences.

- If I recognise and clear up old cross-border experiences in the history of my life, I come considerably closer to my personal life goal with regards to partnership.

- I therefore accept the "invitation" of the person who fails to give way to me as a helpful impulse for the discovery of similar and much older stories which are not completely cleared up yet. The memory is the true gift of that encounter for me. Wishing them a pleasant journey is my gratitude for it in advance.

If, to stay with this example, you get frequent cross-border invitations and you cannot think of any unclarified experiences in your life story, there is bound to be a blind spot in this story. Allow yourself to feel this real-

isation as a gift and seed in yourself. I would specifically like to recommend that you to read the following
part carefully in case of "blind spots".

Those who understand
what separates them
do not have to separate themselves
from what they do not understand.

The dream of a happy partnership often leads to great chaos with confusing feelings. This often leads to us wishing we could start all over again from the very beginning.

Why not?
Let us start with the dream from the very beginning.
Let us start with A.
Are you ready?

DREAM A

As sad
as only a child can be –
brave
out of sympathy;
in innocence
carrying the same fear
as the person
who died in it.
Helplessly trying
to remember
or in the night,
when dream A
makes the heart beat wildly in panic,
the child seeks
its whole life long
the truth,
the light
and its own
adult self.

06/08/2007

Surprised?

Yes! We discover another secret of karmic relationships.

TRAUMA

Part 5: The Secret Key – Dreams - TRAUMA and Sexuality

Each karmic relationship is shaped by many traumatic events throughout which leave profound turmoil in the soul. Each experience of a traumatic event is accompanied by a psychological split whereby the traumatised part has to be "left behind" in order to ensure survival. Although the surviving part generally prevents us from remembering the bad things that we have experienced, for our protection, we nonetheless encounter this mental split in later life, in the mirror of our Self and in all forms of relationships.

At closer inspection, the experience of a partnership that we perceive or have perceived as imperfect or unhappy therefore often points to a previously experienced, still unprocessed trauma. The gulf created by each separation indicates a much older split within ourselves. According to the latest advances of trauma research by Prof Dr Franz Ruppert there are essentially 5 types of traumas:

- **Existential trauma** (especially marked by fears of death)

- **Loss trauma** (loss of beloved people and important attachment figures, fears of being abandoned)

- **Bonding trauma** (confusion of feelings, disappointed love, rage ...)

- **Bonding system trauma** is usually created within the family system and earlier generations by suppressed incest, murder and other immoral acts in the family. Formation of bonds between victims and perpetrators within a system by means of shame and feelings of guilt, threats, silence and secrets.

- **Symbiosis trauma** is created for example when someone is tied to the traumatic feelings of other persons, grows up with the traumatic feelings of close contacts. If for example a mother is not able to care for her child because of consequences of her own trauma, a child tries to take on the mother's traumatic feelings in order to unburden her. This often starts as early as during pregnancy. This symbiosis trauma enables mother and child to survive.

Little attention is being paid in this context to the traumatic experiences from "previous lives" stored in the soul. This may be due to the fact that in order to conduct such research, you have to leave the classical scientific field and may consider additional factors that come from the fields of spirituality and quantum physics, which are still in the early stages of research. Trauma research itself is also still in its infancy and has more than enough to do with just "this life". Therefore, with the inclusion of "past lives", the task becomes much more complex and requires extensive experience with regards to this sensitive issue. Perhaps we may simply just look closely enough in this life in order to clear up the "heritage from past lives". It will probably be a focus of my studies over the next few years to do more research into this.

From my previous therapeutic practice and own life history it has already become clear that partners in karmic relationships who are marked by traumatic events from "earlier lives" are also heavily burdened by traumatic structures in this life and this current incarnation. A closer look at the childhood and life story of both partners reveals psychological splits which cannot be remembered consciously anymore, caused by various forms of traumas which also originate from the family system. These are often experiences such as

- Violence in the family

- The loss of other siblings, also twins in the womb

- Attempted murder by mother and / or father

- Sexual abuse as well as a father or other parents who have been kept secret

- Pre- or postnatal life threat, life-threatening birth

- Finding the early death of a parent, orphanage, foster parents as an origin – The list could be continued endlessly.

For many children, the mother / father / relatives are like nuclear power stations – the bigger the distance, the better the chances of survival.

You have the feeling that it is dangerous as long as they exist; and what they leave behind will concern many generations yet. "Accidents" are hushed up or "were not so bad". Trust your instinct, even if many people downplay a lot of things.

Distance is often the beneficial consequence of common sense.

My main concern here is not so much the guilt of others, but rather to assist you in taking responsibility for leaving your own "victimhood", without whitewashing the truths of life. I would also like to support you in developing a healthy feeling for the truths in your own life.

In terms of partnership it is important to recognise the affinity to "danger spots" in their origin and to redeem them in love. The more this work is done, the more you will become a magnet that attracts your ideal partner in love.

The greater the chaos in your relationships still is, the less order you have put into your personal life story so far.

The bigger your perceived distance to your dream partner still is, the less responsibility you have taken for truth, clarity and love in relationships of all kinds so far. In any case it becomes clear how helpful it can be to examine and change your approach as well as previous helpers.

Perhaps you are now wondering whether you are affected by the issue of TRAUMA, or perhaps you are already certain of it. A definite indicator for a previous traumatic experience is mental confusion. Therefore, it is **helpful to know that confusion is often the healthiest possible way to draw attention to mental splits in a person.**

Perhaps your life is full of contradictions, inconsistencies and "books with seven seals". You cannot remember large parts of your childhood or you have completely blocked out certain areas of it. For example, in your mind, you can see only the door to a room, but you no longer remember what lay behind it. You can however give a detailed description of other parts of the same apartment.

Note:
The mercy of a trauma lies in forgetting.
The salvation from our nightmares lies in remembering.

This process of remembering should be accompanied in a professional, attentive and loving way. The appreciation and inclusion of the survival part and its protective functions is also of great importance, without which life with the traumatic experience might often find an early end in madness or death. Therefore, if necessary, trust your confusion, conflicting emotions and painful body signals. Look at it as a healthy cry for help by the lost parts of your soul, which, as if buried in a tunnel, place all hope in you with unwavering faith. Your shining soul will only make all these things light up in your life until you courageously follow the signs and begin the rescue operation. I wish you good luck with that even now.

If you recognise yourself in this guide and have the feeling that you have lost something important in a karmic relationship, you will probably find yourself again, along with many answers and insights, in modern trauma therapy according to Prof Dr Franz Ruppert. No matter what happened: You are worthy of love. Respect the signs of your partnerships and separations. Follow the footsteps of your relationships to the origin of your destiny. Start in this life.

Do you consider yourself important enough as a human being and soul to set off on this journey? I hope and wholeheartedly wish that the revelation of this further mystery of karmic relationships activates enough hope and courage in you to fight for what love in its most beautiful form was always willing to give: Freedom!

Sometimes it is good to stop and reflect for a moment, but whenever you feel reluctant, fearful or doubtful - remember these words:

The paths of escape and forgetting become tighter and more impassable with each year.
In the dead-end at the end of their lives, for some people there is often only one thing left to be forgotten along this path: their name.

In medicine, the symptoms of this last **vanishing point** would be referred to as **dementia**.
Perhaps you should note it down while you still remember.

There is space for it here:
Your first name
Your surname

I know you are probably not affected by this but I would like to mention it here for the sake of completeness, clarity and for better understanding of other people:

Each remedy that helps you to forget about physical (pain of any sort ...) or psychological (depression etc.) symptoms naturally leads to the same vanishing point of mental derangement in the long term, because that's where the shadows are greatest.

As long as the consequences of trauma and its symptoms are diagnosed and catalogued as a disease, the trauma itself does not need to be treated. Economically, this is a very successful method in securing patients for the duration of their lifetimes who never really become healthy. And this of course also perfectly supports our own survival mechanisms which distract us from ever recognising and naming the true cause.

Anyone who has not really looked during his lifetime, who never really wanted to see the truth, will look into the mirror of truth at the end of life without seeing or understanding it. For many people the truth thus remains in the dark as desired, since the soul simply turns the light off at some point. Everything is forgotten until a new day dawns, in another incarnation. Only the soul remembers and the body feels the pain of old wounds. Very quickly, the "new life" adds similar new wounds, for the soul is still entangled with its karmic relationship to life. I hope you will use this life right now, because you have probably never been so close to the truth of your personal karmic history.

Ideally you have a partner by your side who like you is willing to look at his own psychical splits and traumas and to cure them. In mutual understanding, a deep love can help to master such great challenges in a healthy way. Please do not hurry on this journey. Trauma therapy is a path of small, secure steps. This is not due to the inability of therapists but to the special security mechanisms of the trauma structures. The path follows an inner logic which quickly gives rise to hope and courage to carry on. Even if you do not always understand all the individual steps, you can feel the power which leads to more clarity and truth.

Patience is rewarded along this way with a new sense of yourself and of life.

Here, modern trauma therapy and trauma constellation can make a major contribution.

TRAUMA and External Energy

Traumatic structures have very strong similarities with magical and ritual bonds such as curses and others. If you still have the feeling that everything is "jinxed" after ritual release attempts in this context, I would definitely recommend trauma therapy for you. If external energies exist in your life there are probably traumas caused by external influence which have not or not yet been worked through completely.

Some trauma structures may appear in your life as "demons" – "lost souls" or other forms of external energies. I have also been confronted by soul parts split by TRAUMA in form of "external energy". Since we are often separated from such soul parts for decades, it is completely normal and logical that these parts seem alien to us! It is not quite like that in reverse, but similar. Most of the split soul parts know that they belong to us, but they often show themselves as really aggressive, hurt, angry and mistrustful because they believe we had abandoned them on purpose and left them behind deliberately. Why is that the case?

Soul parts split off by TRAUMA know practically nothing about the rest of the further life after the traumatic event. Their development has been halted and they feel like a child left alone somewhere in a big supermarket. Deep sadness and depression are often the waves of despair and distress this "child" feels who is still alive but has been separated from you since then and with whom you still have a connection through this TRAUMA. That's why it is often necessary to take several steps in gradually getting to know each other and building trust, before a complete "reunification" can be carried out.

The Truth about the Myth of Dual Souls

In the so-called "spiritual" and "esoteric" scene, there is a theme which is often discussed but rarely well explained and which you have probably also encountered already: Dual souls. In short, according to the dual soul theory, there is another part of us somewhere in the form of another person with whom we could enter into the ideal of all possible partnerships – provided we find this second part of us in any life. With luck, perhaps even in this one.

So far, so good. Admittedly, this is a very romantic idea. What is it like in practice though, and what can we learn from life?

Let us lift the romantic veil and uncover the mystery of dual souls! If the theory is right, then why do relationships often fail or even not take place, where a partner believes to have found their "dual soul"? Interested? I will tell you.

For example, you encounter a person as a partner with similar splits in their soul or personality as you have and who therefore seems to be very familiar to you. Partnership is not possible here, because neither can replace their respective parts that have been split off! This illusion is destroyed repeatedly on a "divine level" and by the resistance of our own soul fragment to which we have lost contact, so that no one stops searching for the "true" second part of their own personality.

> ## Note:
> The soul fragment abandoned by us which is calling for help and rebellious, as well as the soul fragment of the other partner will do whatever is necessary to prevent us from uniting with the wrong "dual soul".
>
> **The dual soul we are searching for is a soul fragment which has split off from ourselves!**

Whenever you think that you have met your dual soul in the form of another human being, life will teach you a lesson. Phenomena as described here in this guide will govern your life until you embark on a serious search for the true dual soul fragment. If one day you can embrace your own soul fragment again that has been split off by trauma, you will understand why I am only too happy to bring this illusion of classical dual soul theory back down on earth.

I suspect that this theory was developed by people who were already seeking for a lost fragment which had been separated from them but who were as yet unable to recognise the connection to their own trauma.

184

Point of Reference:
In a separation following a karmic relationship you do not lose your "dual soul" but rather a person with a similarly heavy fate, whose traumatic structures are very similar to your own. As a "double pack", such a meeting often leads, besides the element of fascination, to lots of grief, sorrow, confusion and despair. As long as the traumas are not understood and solved, happiness will be rare here and of short duration.

In order to clear up partnership fate, two different souls meet again and again in new constellations over many lifetimes. The mutually strong attraction is primarily caused by unexplained common destiny and self-created, eternal bonds such as oaths, vows and promises of eternal love and fidelity, which last to this day. This community of fate often loses access to unconditional love and is, despite attraction, fascination and great familiarity, instead increasingly confronted by one's own un-freedom, the true origin of which is no longer remembered. The phenomena of this karmic relationship usually remain a mystery for those affected and many consultants.

In my opinion, ignorance of the true facts gave rise to the description of a relationship image which in the term dual or twin soul has found a theory and classification that is neither accurate nor helpful for those affected. I am speaking about karmic relationships here and would like to invite you to distance yourself from any fixations on a dual soul you might have. This model binds you to a dependency that does not correspond to your divine freedom.

Unfortunately, many spiritual advisors, mediums, clairvoyants and fortune-tellers are not aware of the psychological conflicts they cause for customers and clients when they refer to their partners in relationships and separations as dual or twin souls. For those affected, this means that they are not just dealing with the break-up of a karmic relationship, but also losing the only true and a possible way to experience ultimate happiness. What remains is a customer for the abovementioned group of advisors who is very loyal and desperate for advice.

Allow me to ask you the following questions:
Does this concept really serve your personal independence and freedom?
How much longer do you want to be the victim of a myth which the inventors themselves have not fully understood?
You'll be better off trusting your own feeling. If you feel that there is something that is separated from you and belongs to you, you can assume that this has nothing to do with another person or dual soul. Enjoy the thought that the fine tie between you and one of your split soul parts still exists and is palpable. In such circumstances it is well worth going into your own responsibility with all your strength and stamina in or-

der to learn to understand the history of your split soul with a person you trust and to bring it into a new, beneficial order.

Note:
The classic dual soul theory is a classic escape projection onto another level (another partner, another dimension ...) due to a lack of other insights. In its true core it contains the theme of the splitting and separation from another part of the soul, the "dual soul". But as often happens in real life, it is nobody but ourselves who we may encounter in the end. The real secret of dual souls emerges as the search for a part of our own soul, split off by trauma.

This view does not entail the risk of an unhappy fixation on something unattainable. It provides a comprehensive framework and a new bearing for your life which is entirely under your control. Are you really ready for it?

If you want to follow my observations, they will lead you to a new opportunity to design the freedom of your life. It entails very different chances to meet a partner with whom you may spend the best time of your life. The happiness in the relationship is determined here by your own inner wholeness.

Identity Confusions, Twins and Excessive Demands on Partners

People who are flooded with their parents' traumatic feelings from as early as their time in the womb and are thus forced to assimilate them as their own feelings invariably find it very difficult later to determine who they really are and what they really want in life. Before they can clearly decide on a life partner who really fits their own needs, it is necessary to resolve the feelings and identities mixed up with those of the parents. When you notice that your partner is more mommy's or daddy's little darling than your love and happiness, it is high time for you to become suspicious.

It means that you have chosen a partner with the identity parts that stem from your mother or your father. The part of yourself that is the real you was possibly not even involved in the choosing of your partner or had only the limited voice of a child who even as an adult still wants to be mommy's or daddy's favourite!

With twins it is often the case that each of the twins considers the other as their own ego or a part of it. This naturally raises fears of being incomplete and not being able to live without the other twin. These fears are later sometimes transferred onto the partner as well who generally ends up completely overwhelmed by this. Again, it is important for both twins to develop a sense of their own unrelated identity and existence. Twins must develop a clear reference to themselves as independent beings, otherwise they run the risk of marrying a partner who is actually a better fit for the other twin. This is because subconsciously, the still mixed twin identity is trying to continue the twin symbiosis with a partner and thereby attracts a partner who corresponds to the other twin. However, this rarely leads to lasting happiness because the part that is the twin's actual own identity quite rightly feels betrayed here.

Other aspects regarding twins:

- Twins "create" a counterpart so that at least one is there – if the neglect by the parents ("no time", overwhelmed etc.) already seems inevitable.

- Twins "create" a counterpart because they would not be able to survive in the family system into which they were born – here, the twin often becomes the "knowing witness" of traumatic events and a helping straw to grasp in order to survive.

During my further studies into trauma constellation, an interesting thought was expressed which I would like to share with you here. Identical twins may already experience a separation in the womb because the deluge of the mother's traumatic feelings leads to a separation. The topic of psychological separation and trauma is thus practically put into their cradle. The mother's inner spiritual separation practically becomes evident and visible from the outside, in the form of her children. It is however also continued this way, generally without really being recognised.

One cannot generalise of course, but I do know twins where this is actually the case. If you are a twin child yourself, these clues you might have found you your "needle in a haystack" and thus another "aha-moment".

Above all, I want to show you how complex psychological and interpersonal entanglements can be, even before the topics of love and partnership start to play a role in your consciousness. The way your outlook on life was shaped before your first breath and from then onwards is therefore of essential importance for your future happiness in love. **The tragedy of a karmic relationship often has its origin in a forgotten tragedy in childhood.** Your string of unhappy relationships will hopefully soon find a happy ending with the help of the impulses in this guide, even if these impulses are "only" the seeds for the fruits that you still have to work towards.

"Karmic Relationship" with a Twin Lost in the Womb

In recent years scientific studies have shown that many people have already lost their twin in the womb without ever knowing anything about it. Even if doctors or midwives see that there was someone else there, they unfortunately usually hide this – mostly out of misplaced consideration. Here we encounter another karmic relationship with shared hard fate which is usually concealed. This loss is often also reflected in partnerships, until the surviving twin has recognised and dealt with the origin of his misfortune.

The vital work on mourning and "correction" of the family system is especially important for the affected twins so that they are able to allow themselves a new life and love without guilt so that they no longer have to use partnerships to create new separations over and over again in order to be "close" to the lost twin through the pain. It is also important here to recognise the mother as part of this karmic relationship and to include her in the work-up. Often there are unconscious accusations and blame placed on the mother.

<u>Possible Clues for a Twin Lost in the Womb:</u>

- No matter how wonderful your partner is, you always have the feeling that something is missing.

- You work for two but you have the feeling to earn only half a wage.

- When reading books or watching movies about re-connecting / reuniting families, unusually strong feelings stir inside you.

- You should actually be happy but your depression and inner longing for something unknown to you is accompanying you persistently, like a sad, dark shadow.

- You have been feeling guilty for as long as you can remember but you do not know why.

- Something in you blames your mother but there is no visible reason for it.

- Again and again you have the feeling that there is an unspoken secret between you and your mother.

Do you want to know more about it? **Here is a book recommendation:** *The Drama in the Womb* by Alfred R. and Bettina Austermann, Königsweg Verlag, 2006

Perhaps your mother's or grandparents' siblings have also been lost or aborted and you do not know anything about them. This can generate similar feelings as clues.

No partner can share a feeling of happiness with you which you cannot yet allow yourself because a part of you is still caught up in the pain and shock of the loss of your twin. To witness its twin's death is a traumatic experience for the soul. The emotional entanglement with another unborn or prematurely deceased sibling can have a similar impact. Since this is difficult to verify, there is a danger that an illusory story might be used to satisfy the deep longing and desire not to be alone anymore. To create this "ideal world" in classic family constellation, sometimes people have to make do with an "illusionary twin" due to the absence of other answers. Everyone is happy because they want to believe in this solution and nobody realises that this "presumed twin" does not exist in reality. This risk in experimental procedures is often underestimated. I would therefore recommend that you check such results before you internalise the corresponding solution.

Here, the "problem" is not the twin as such but the often still existing TRAUMA due to the loss. You can only find out whether your life and partnership problems are really connected to this theme by checking whether a loss / bonding trauma concerning your twin really exists and to what extent you are affected by it. Most "constellation experts" and therapists however are not trained to do this.

Some people also invent a lie to keep living; but mostly a bad taste remains and life happiness remains incomplete. Lies, stories and fantasies of a healthy world are parts of a survival mechanism which is used to shape the truth so that we can draw new strength from it. You should always be aware of this. This part much prefers to follow an illusion than to get to the core of a painful truth.

I do not know which information in this guide is actually important for you and what hidden truths form the basis of your life. Simply trust your emotional reactions to certain information and follow these feelings to the origin of the truth connected with them. Follow a healthy, critical approach and do not let anybody talk you into things you do not really feel.

Point of Reference:
Methods and techniques are only useful when researching your own life truths if they serve your soul. The "spirit" loves to run away with mental techniques and often does not notice that it has left the soul behind. Your soul knows the truth and your body as a vessel is always in resonance with it. Therefore, signals by your body always lead you to truths and still hidden secrets of your life.

Never

How can it be,
I ask myself.
How can parents
allow
and do this?

Never
does the child
cry inside me
and yet
the body twitches
in the night,
when it
remembers.

21/12/2009

Dreams – Trauma and Sexuality

Wherever someone was traumatised by sexual abuse, dreams can often appear, frequently with sexual, often confusing content which touches on something prohibited. This is often very irritating and incomprehensible, especially if we are in a sexually fulfilled relationship. The same thing of course also applies to experiences of violence, sadism, cruelty and the like.

The following information might perhaps help you to consider your own experiences in a new context and to choose new ways to achieve a greater personal freedom by discovering the truth about your childhood.

In order to better understand yourself and these complex connections you should be aware of the following facts beforehand:

A child has to see everything it has experienced through or with significant persons as "good" and accept it in love because anything else would mean a threat to its life. In its helplessness and dependency a child would hardly survive the truth of violence and sexual abuse. Even as adults we need assistance, help and "witnesses" in order to get to the truths about familial taboos and our own traumas.

Maybe you, as a man, have dreams in which you exchange caresses with your sister / brother / male friend / unknown man, you are strongly sexually aroused and experience this sexuality to the point of physical union with orgasm and enjoy it despite your irritation.

Maybe you, as a woman, have dreams in which you exchange caresses with your brother / sister / female friend / unknown woman, you are sexually strongly aroused and experience this sexuality to the point of physical union with orgasm and enjoy it despite your irritation.

Here the following possible correlations can be significant:

- Your dreams remind you of a very intensive, also sexual relationship with a person from a previous life who you have met again in this life – in another constellation. This hints at a classic form of karmic relationship with all associated learning tasks and possibilities. The truth of this version can be clarified through regression but it should always be checked against real childhood experiences from this life in order to prevent an escape projection to other worlds or lives.

- As a child you experienced the rape of your mother or your mother was already traumatised by rape before the pregnancy with you – perhaps you are the result of rape. You have thus grown up in the trauma of your mother and have stored this memory. You are basically a raped child and carry the rapist's energy inside you (victim and perpetrator structure).

- During pregnancy you were already overwhelmed by your parents' traumatic feelings which they might even have taken on from their parents (your grandparents).

- As a child you experienced your father being raped.

- As a child you experienced your sister / your brother being sexually abused.

- You have been sexually abused yourself and have learned to leave your body (dissociation) in order not to feel it. In your memory it is so as if "it" was happening to someone else.

If it becomes unbearable to feel our own emotions, we remove ourselves from them internally. Powerlessness and dissociation are two well-known surviving mechanisms which you are most likely also familiar with. Once this protective function has been activated, another "survival system" kicks in to focus all attention and perception on the environment, the situation, the threat, the feelings of perpetrators, etc. We are devoid of any emotion ourselves, but our "radar system" makes us feel everything else very intensively. This is the only chance to find a solution or to recognise when the danger is over.

Since we pretty much cut ourselves off from the events, only "the other" remains visible and palpable in later memory. This leads to years of emotional turmoil, sensations and dreams which we do not understand.

If you have experienced a traumatising event yourself, this may have the effect in later relationships that for example you develop a stronger connection with the feelings and traumatised parts of your partner (mutual attraction) than with your own feelings. Misunderstandings and difficulties are inevitable this way. You may feel for example what another person's traumatised parts would need right now and therefore you have great difficulties to get closer erotically. Other times this may be exactly the opposite. There are of course many variations.

Why do your dreams often show situations that did not happen this way and do not correspond to your desires either?
Why do you appear as an active person in the dream who is enjoying something that you would never do in reality?
Why do you experience the pictures and physical feelings in such a real and intensive way?

You were there "live" or have experienced it in very intensive empathy. Through one of your caregivers from your childhood (father, mother, uncle, aunt ...) you have immersed yourself completely in this situation or stored memory and therefore experience this situation in your dreams today in such a realistic way as if you, rather than the caregiver, had been the active person. Even your physical sensations can be dominated by the same intense pleasure that one of your close contacts had experienced back then. Since a child's observation is almost always complete, intense and unfiltered, the child's imagination does not separate between the observed and the experienced event. The special connection with close contacts intensifies this impression even further. Here we can see a complex mixture of shock, confusion and fascination. Frequently this results in irrational feelings of guilt about not having prevented the event from happening, or even worse, the idea of being the initiator or the cause one-self.

The fact that the affected person is unable to turn off these sexual dreams is later often accompanied by their own feelings of shame and guilt when the enjoyment of the power of sexual excitement, nudity and sexual union is undeniable despite all the irritation.

Additionally, there is also the phenomenon where many people learn to leave their body in life-threatening situations so as not to have to feel the other's violence towards their body. In these people's memory of it is often as if "it" had happened to someone else. The threatening event is experienced from the position of an observer or is completely repressed by means of psychological flight into a fantasy world.

A single child has no siblings as compassionate witnesses by its side and often blames itself for the "punishment" and torture by others. Every child thus develops its own strategies to survive and to explain its experience. Do you already have an idea how you survived your "happy childhood"?

If you tell me a little more about yourself, I can help you to figure it out. There is one thing I can tell you with confidence and let you take on your way with you right now though. The little child you were then did not have any structures to enable it to classify this event which had been repeating for years. The fact that your caregiver could do such things is also so incredible and life-threatening that it must be completely deleted from your world and imagination. This is a protective function and a survival mechanism.

What remains, for example, is the memory of your love for your sister / your brother and your whole sexual experience with that person. In a child's classification, a couple-relationship between adult siblings develops from this through dreams as the only possible "acceptable" connection. This also touches on a prohibition but does not threaten the dependence on the early childhood caregiver.

In addition, perpetrators mentally often raise the victims of their abuse to the status of a sexually mature person before the act. In order to basically grant themselves the legitimacy for rape, some perpetrators develop the fantasy that they are just fulfilling the desire of the victim to be introduced into the practice of sexuality. In their imagination and the experience of some perpetrators, the victim therefore has fun in this illicit sexual encounter. Due to the intense contact with perpetrator energy, your dreams can therefore reflect mutual joy in the forbidden sex with a brother, sister or mother from an adult's perspective.

A child cannot distinguish between intense fantasy and reality and therefore experiences this perpetrator energy unfiltered as an adult. Therefore, do not be afraid to talk frankly about your dreams with someone you trust who is familiar with these topics. You may even have some old diary entries about it.

Discussion therapy alone does not help though, because this is about mental confusion and split by TRAUMA.

What can you do in such a case right now in order to get these images "out of your head"? The information so far has already had a positive clearing effect on your subconscious. In addition, you can do the following – I will limit myself here to the example of sexualised dreams with siblings. Imagine a picture of your sister / brother as best you can – maybe you even have a photo.

Then address that person aloud:
"Dear .... I am your brother / sister .... and not like – dad / mom / uncle / aunt - / - neighbour – the person who sexually abused you when you were a child.

What – XY / *someone from our family* – that person did to you has given a sexual character to our relationship, in my dreams as well.

I love you as a brother / sister, but not sexually. This is not a part of the two of us. This has been confusing me for a long time. Only now can I see clearly what happened. I have probably not coped with the truth before. We are brother and sister/ - brothers / sisters, but not a couple. I no longer have to use this lie to cover up those bad things that happened to you / to us."

Just follow your instincts and if necessary develop your own sentences to provide solutions. You cannot go far wrong there. If the sentences are not correct, they will not work as a solution. Your body will react with relaxation and deeper breathing and your dreams will change. You can also deal with other topics in similar ways. Check out my recommendations for modern trauma therapy.

Other phenomena:

If sons learn from their father / grandfather / uncle that sexual exploitation is normal, they soon become perpetrators just like their role models and can sexually exploit their own sister/s and younger brothers without questioning this assumption. They simply follow the example of their role model in an attempt to be a "man" in a similar manner. Under certain circumstances this might therefore result in a person being abused by several other people in the family. Consequently even children can become perpetrators against their own siblings, classmates or children from the neighbourhood. Depending on the behaviour patterns of the role model / models, children may beat, humiliate, disparage, blackmail or abuse. The principle is always similar. Since children are proud to be like their role models it is also difficult to change these copied behaviours later. Features of the adult personality which imitate the behaviour of role models and perpetrators from early childhood are connected through this copied "lifestyle" of the caregiver from early childhood. Therefore, as a rule, punishment alone does not help the perpetrators to break those patterns of behaviour permanently. Prison confinement is like a "loyalty test" and is usually a price paid willingly for love and child-like longing for a connection which has been subconscious, misunderstood and unconditional from the very beginning. From this infantile point of view no punishment can be greater than the fear of losing this bond. Even the affected person's own talents and life are often sacrificed to this bond.

Victims also often imitate their perpetrators, albeit unconsciously. For example, they develop so-called self-punishment mechanisms, the structure of which is rarely obvious to affected persons. Essentially, every action is related to the bond from early childhood and confirms it.

People say: "Children forget so fast" – is that really true? Let us take a closer look at the possible consequences of a sexualised childhood. Terms and texts can be varied.

17 Possible Sexual Behaviour Patterns as a Consequence of a Sexualised Childhood

If necessary, replace sex by violence ... and adjust the examples accordingly. Take advantage of the orientation and develop your own list.

Since children feel connected to siblings and adult caregivers with equal intensity, their trauma feelings and dreams also mix. One's own experience with these traumatic mixtures and interpretations can later lead to the fact...

- ...that you start to have sexual experiences with many different persons from a very early age, so that your "first experience" remains only one of many.

- ...that you might subconsciously try to wash the seed of your father / uncle / brother out of your body with the seed of many other men in order to get rid of the pictures and feelings from that time.

- ...that you enjoy (compulsively need) someone else to watch you during sex (the same way as your brother / sister / mother ... did or were forced to do against their will when you were being abused in the past).

- ...that you enjoy watching yourself during sex – using mirrors or a camera –, the same way as you did as a child after you learned to leave your body during abuse.

- ...that you can't have light or music on during sex with a partner because you were completely alone with "all that" back then and silence and darkness come closest to that.

- ...that you experience your sexuality in your completely "silent world" because perhaps during your abuse you were forced to "keep silent", with a hand in front of your mouth under threat to your life – even today, an ecstatic, passionate enjoyment of your sexuality is still beyond your imagination because you could only survive by keeping quiet back then. If your neighbour can hear you while cleaning your teeth rather than while having a passionate orgasm then maybe a part of your personal and also sexual freedom is still locked up in your early childhood or youth.

- ...that you unconsciously seek an older person as your first partner because this corresponds to your experience from childhood. Maybe you keep this pattern for the rest of your life without questioning it or finding adequate answers.

- ...that you look for partners who are to do with "law" or "public relations work" in order to unconsciously make up for your childhood right to protection, defence and publication of what was done to you. Here, the part of you which is the child looking for protection and is still stuck in TRAUMA is looking for the partner.

- …that passion in relationships is more important to you than love – this way a part of you is trying to remind you of the fact that there is still something that creates suffering – the typical suffering in such relationships mostly isn't understood or researched further so that it often requires many repetitions of passionate and sorrowful relationships to recognise that here is "something" wrong other than the partner.

- …that you try to flee out of the sexual role you were born into.

- …that sexuality for you is possible/comfortable only with a partner of the same sex because you observed yourself during your abuse and remember this as a different person of the same sex. Since you had to delete the other sex of your caregiver from early childhood from your mind and your imagination of sexuality, the mark of intensive sexual delight with a person of the same sex remains stored (via the childish identification with the observed rapist) in your inner world as a "legitimate" option. Later, this leads you to the desire to repeat this form of sexuality and enjoyment.

> ## Point of Reference:
> **A sexual preference for same-sex love can arise from the experience of sexual abuse in early childhood.**

Those who as children observed themselves in a psychological split during an act of abuse will later no longer associate this with themselves but with a stranger ("it is not happening to me – protection").

This "act of love" which takes place with another person of the same sex is invariably stored as some kind of first "sexual reference". By characterising it as "good" the survival Self even lifts the experience to a "highlight". In retrospect, the acceptance of the bad thing as something good turns out to be the only possible way to survive this bad time.

If you live in a same sex relationship, you may have thought about the possibility that earlier encounters in other lives may be the reason for it. This is possible of course. In order to exclude the possibility that you are trying to avoid another truth with this idea, I recommend you perform a detailed and careful examination of your childhood story. Maybe your purportedly "karmic relationship" turns out to be a pure survival strategy.

208

As an adult you are only free to decide on the form of your sexuality if you realised, understood and worked through the truth about the influences on your early childhood.

- ...that you later convert the powerlessness you felt in early childhood by exercising in and with sexuality the power which you did not have then. Maybe you do the same or similar things today as you did as a child (oral sex ...) but this time you do it with the feeling of temptation and power. You dominate the others and make them "dance to your tune". Perhaps this gives you the feeling of getting over the helplessness from that time (when you were forced as a child). But the childhood split remains until your own experience of abuse has been resolved.

- ...that you later use sexuality to manipulate other people in order to make them pay for your injuries from early childhood. You use your partners like "disposable items" to get even with the opposite sex. The love in your heart remains cold. The more the people you leave or throw out suffer the better.

- ...that your life is marked by the "payment by others" for your services in sexuality (body, voice, film).

- ...that you unconsciously search for a partner who later abuses your children.

- ...that you try to avoid partnerships of any kind for a long time because you suspect but do not know what happened to you in your childhood. Just like this topic, a partner is unimaginable and sometimes remains a taboo for your entire lifetime.

- As an adult you might perhaps develop the desire to be tied up or beaten by your partner during sex because this raises your sexual arousal or reaching an orgasm is possible for you only with this "support". Maybe you are time after time unconsciously recreating the violent events from your own childhood experience as well as your inability to act back then. Through your sex partner you feel the passion of the former perpetrator which has unconsciously become your own.

These are possible explanations for circumstances which may still have an influence on your life today, in one way or another, because your sexual experience in early childhood has led to psychological confusion and psychological splits. The list serves only as orientation and does not claim to be complete. The imprints caused by such events make fulfilled sexuality and genuine love seem irreconcilable.

Even if you lack personal memories, there are certain signs that can help you recognise the consequences of traumas.

35 Possible Signs of Trauma

- You can neither laugh nor cry.

- Other people's happiness and luck make you sad or angry.

- You have built up a physically visible protective wall but you do not know exactly why.

- It is easier to cry about other people's suffering than about your own.

- The love that others show to you hurts you because consciously or unconsciously it awakens the memory of something "old" that urgently needed such love but never got it. Therefore, in your current world every sign of love from other people practically comes "too late". Unconsciously you avoid any form of such feelings, you do not let them happen, do not let them affect you.

- No matter how hard you try, nothing in your life is truly successful.

- Every "positive" flow in life is quickly nipped in the bud.

- You feel like you've been ordered but not picked up, literally "as if rooted to the spot" in life because you seemingly cannot change anything no matter how hard you try.

- You always encounter life itself and other people as "spoilsports".

- You feel torn between love, life and death.

- You keep turning into the "perpetrator" without really wanting it or being able to prevent it.

- You have nightmares although you are no fan of scary movies.

- You often feel pain in your heart, medically everything seems to be alright though.

- You often suffer from some kind of physical pain, medically everything seems to be alright though.

- To your surprise, some passages in books or particular film scenes distress/touch you unusually deeply – something in you reacts spontaneously.

- Speechlessness and inability to speak.

- Emotional distress and helplessness when meeting other people.

- You are often mentally "absent", you "beam" yourself away without noticing it yourself and other people struggle to get you back. If somebody speaks to you, you do not react or react only with great effort.

- Often you look through other people as if they were only air / transparent.

- You are always perceived as indifferent by others.

- If you drive your car you are often miles away in your thoughts, fall asleep although you have slept well. Often you do not even know how you managed to arrive at your destination without getting into an accident.

- You feel overwhelmed and confused by events and inconsistencies in your life.

- You do not have any feeling for what you want or what is right for you anymore.

- Wrong decisions seem to be right to you. You know that something is not good for you but you do it anyway.

- You are always the target of massive bullying "below the belt".

- You suffer from extreme fear, aggression, panic attacks.

- Energies of self-destruction, sabotage and accidents are obvious in your life.

- You take antidepressants and similar drugs in order not to feel something (what?). With that you separate yourself from the last cries for help by your split soul fragments and deepen your own estrangement. Depression instead of reaction.

- You are touched and fascinated by the dual soul theory and similar things, saying that there is an ideal soul partner who was lost some day, and with whom it would be the greatest luck for you to "merge".

- You start new projects full of enthusiasm but you do not continue them or abort them if they are successful.

- You have already forgotten what you read on the last pages here. It is as if somebody has erased all footprints "behind you" in your memory. You notice your severe forgetfulness, the effort it takes to concentrate and even "blackouts", or other people draw your attention to these issues.

- For years you have been living in circumstances which overburden you and feel that it is beyond you to change anything. This is a possible indication of a survival strategy which was fixed by a childhood trauma and observes in rigid inability to act and lets everything happen in order to survive.

- Although there is enough time to act you cannot do it. You feel as if paralysed, frozen, hypnotised or narcotised.

- You do not know why, but you have never been able to build up a relationship of trust with your parents – and on top of that you may feel guilty about it as well.

- A mixture of overload, confusion and disorientation leads for example to you misplacing or forgetting items. The "good" is thrown away, the "bad" is kept. You leave rubbish, socks or car keys in the refrigerator.

It's good if you can laugh about that. If you learn to understand it you can change it.

Some Characteristic Features of Trauma in Keywords

- Frequently drifting away, mental absence, disorientation, confusion

- Tiredness, falling asleep unintentionally, being as if under anaesthetic, high blood pressure, burn-out

- Isolation, speechlessness – inner block stopping you from speaking, insensitivity

- Always the same problems - neighbours, finances, partner, pain, stress, addictions, eating disorder...

- Tendency to suffer accidents, injuries, illnesses, overburdening, dissociation

- External energies, external control, feeling of external control, "voices in the head"

- Fear of lifts, metro or other people, no sense of danger

- Avoiding physical contact, closeness, sexuality, even in a partnership

- Forgetfulness, big gaps in memory, sudden loss of one's own thoughts

- Feelings of powerlessness and helplessness – "inability" to react in time

- Tendency towards self-destruction

- We are stuck in our dream (nightmare, life dream).

Trauma and "Trigger"

Sensory impressions such as hearing, smell, seeing or feeling are saved in a fragmented (separated) form during experiences and events which traumatise us.

These sounds, smells, pictures and feelings relating to the trauma are stored under shock and are suppressed. Similar sounds, smells, pictures and feelings can have a "triggering" effect in later life and for example set off feelings of panic. The current situation can be the complete opposite of the feelings set off by it (fear, panic, nausea, dizziness, fainting...). This only becomes clear when we know that the unconscious attribution of the fragmented sensory impressions related to the event which has traumatised us remains with us even if we have forgotten about the event itself.

In order to avoid misunderstandings and conflicts in partnerships and relationships it is helpful and useful to share this basic knowledge with each other. In the interest of all those affected I would like to ask you for one thing here. Do not take any of your counterpart's incomprehensible reactions personally straight off. If you can find a connection to the reaction – a gifted "rose", beginning of music ... – switch off the "trigger" if possible. Help the partner to leave the place, the room, the persons, the situation. Search for professional help together.

Trauma and Physical Symptoms

The longer the energy of trauma is stored in the body, the stronger its physicality will become, meaning it will show itself in physical symptoms. This provides the opportunity to deal with the part of our self which carries the symptom we want to understand and dissolve.

Advice on Dealing with "Psychological" TRAUMA

In simple terms, trauma is to do with the integration of split soul and character fragments. It is about the connection to one's own healthy parts, to which almost all contact has been lost. This is a multi-layered process in which several components play a role. It is helpful to consider the following points here:

- The knowledge of a trauma alone is not sufficient to change the consequences.

- Even the experience of traumatic feelings does not dissolve them.

- You can neither un-create a TRAUMA nor can you handle it like a "stubborn mass" or something similar, even if similar phenomena appear (for all fans of avatar techniques – even for the wizard the right tools are missing here / my state of knowledge 2001).

- A trauma cannot be "outsmarted" by any NLP techniques known to me.

- In connection with trauma, even body-orientated methods only are only useful in the hands of trained and experienced trauma therapists. In all honesty, everything else should be recommended and enjoyed as a "wellness treatment" without therapeutic claim; physical therapy as additional support and accompaniment to trauma therapy can be very helpful in cases of physical pain and trauma-orientated symptoms. From own experience I can particularly recommend Feldenkrais sessions and Craniosacral osteopathy.

Why Do Most Forms of Therapy not Work when it Comes to Dealing with Trauma?

Most techniques essentially only strengthen the survival parts within us and according to my experience they cannot unmake the split caused by trauma.

From my experience, no technique along the lines of "No matter what happened – I will build myself a perfect new world" will be able to fundamentally and permanently solve any of your life problems which are based on a trauma. Even if a friendly thought never hurt anyone – the limits of your happiness in a partnership cannot be expanded permanently with positive thinking alone. The "coming back down to reality" will be harder every time and more frustrating with each "success seminar".

The essence of "at-the-touch-of-a-button" and "push-away" acupuncture techniques is also to strengthen the survival Self – which is of course delighted with any quick solution that promises to swiftly delete a few symptoms, "ideally even before breakfast", and to be able to produce another piece of a perfect world. Depending on the programme, you can also push away other warning signals in your life for a while. Reality will catch up with you sooner or later because no matter how strong your faith and positive thinking may be: with "illusionary oil" in its gearbox, your ship of dreams will soon run aground on the next sandbank. Even if you turn a blind eye to it, you will feel that previous warning signs would have called for a more profound examination of the engine room.

The side effects of symptom-chain treatment with medication inevitably lead to chains of surgical table treatments on a long-term basis. True autonomy and freedom begin when we stop our lifelong concern with "burnout, depression, alcoholism, anorexia, "your symptom",... and start to take a tenacious interest in the deeper causes of our "symptoms". This includes all issues at relationship level.

My recommendation:

Take the carrot away from the donkey and stop deceiving yourself. It is time to hang the "whip" on the wall and to take things a bit easier in the "survival mode". It is time to massively rethink the strategy and to call into question all methods, treatments and techniques used until now. Follow "the cries of your inner child" to the soul fragments which feel abandoned by you and maybe have been waiting for their liberation for decades. Be prepared for resistance and do not waste any time on trying to do this on your own. Creating a fulfilled love relationship in divine freedom and genuine love is no "one man / one woman show".

Because in a child's world it is inexplicable to experience this at the hands of trusted people and thus leads to splits, other people often take the position of the perpetrators in dreams. In order for the child's ideal world not to collapse in the face of life-threatening experiences – due to parents or caregivers – the perpetrators and the experience must be changed through fantasies.

According to personal beliefs, the experience of the trauma is packaged in the most positive way available. Spiritually-orientated people can also include, for example, colouring from previous lives. That way, abuse by a male (a father) might be, after "repackaging", represented as a homosexual relationship in a previous life. There it might even have meant casual fun. In such dreams, male friends from this life are only stand-ins for male caregivers known in childhood. For women this is principally analogous.

Trauma feelings are often even taken on from the parents.

At a time when we do not have a choice (pregnancy) or a possibility to differentiate (baby, child). The trauma feelings of parents might already have been taken over from their ancestors. This leads to identity confusion. Therefore, processing and clarification of trauma can only succeed with the help of multigenerational thinking.

For as long as an experience of abuse / incest / mistreatment is not remembered and processed, it works like an explosive in every relationship. The "Karma" of your "karmic relationship" then arises from this life and has nothing to do with past lives or your common history – even though there may be some such elements.

The "Curse" of Traumas
Traumas that have not been recognised or processed yet can have similar effects to ones we might otherwise only know from "black magic". One's own life seems to be "cursed" forever. Life stands still, often feels like it is set in concrete or permanently leads to new disasters. Our entire lives are accompanied by the feeling that we are not really able to change anything crucial in our life structures. Compared to my

own life, concrete seemed a liquid mass for me for many years.

Note:
A TRAUMA cannot be resolved without being processed.
To process a TRAUMA means to get back in touch with split soul fragments as well as the healthy parts of feelings.
A TRAUMA does not automatically stop simply because you are aware of it.
You cannot bring back the soul fragments and feelings split off by trauma with your intellect or logical reasoning alone.
Professional help is useful here.

If we touch on the topic of injuries we also come in contact with the related sadness which probably still hasn't been given a worthy place to date. In the split-off fragments, all that waits for our loving embrace today.

Below you can find a few poems on the topic of "trauma".

Perhaps one or the other poem will touch on hidden knowledge inside you.

Desire to Have Children

Beyond the lies
there is still air
to breath
and to feel
that the truth
lies deeper
than all those lies can reach.

Your voice quivers
when you say,
everything was normal
with us
back then –
and daddy
did not mean
it that way.

My heart is racing
with fear
that someday
things could be again
as they were before,
the truth is
so normal
inside me,
a truth that even today
still cries for help,
mother.

20/12/2009

Mother

I smile at you
and sense
that you feel easier
in the hope
that everything
will somehow end well
for us.
The nightmare
is breathing down my neck
and the fear of it
paralyses my voice,
the same way as it paralyses the steps
you try to take to save us.

I shiver at the thought
that I have to find
the hope to survive
in myself –
the same way as my sister
whom you had abandoned already
before I was born.

I smile at you
because I sense
that this is the only way
to survive,
as I am much too young
for anything else.

An ice-cold chill runs through me
at the thought of
how carelessly you

have handed over
our young children's souls
to the madness
that we call
"daddy".

01/01/2010

Summary of Part 5:

About the Longing for a Complete Love Relationship

With a traumatic life history you encounter every form of relationship as an incomplete, "damaged" and injured personality with the conscious or unconscious hope to become complete through the current partner. This must always fail because a partner can never substitute one's own split fragments of personality and feelings. The "better half" that many people are searching for is indeed nothing more than their own identity.

So our own experience of deficiency, unhappiness, incomplete love and numbness inevitably continues until we can start to integrate the split parts of our personality again.

The "healthier" we are in our own personality, the more complete our chance will become to be able to love ourselves unconditionally in the mirror of a partner. Any form of deficiency always points to parts of our own divinity which are not available to us because we left them behind at some point or had to "give them up" in order to survive. It is the real challenge and mission of our humanity to regain these parts of our personality.

Partners can help us to pick up the "golden thread" that life offers us in the mirror of the deficiency and misfortune. If your partner makes you feel like a victim, your view is not yet free for the seed which produces the crop that is causing you grief right now. I do not wish to relieve anyone of their responsibility for their actions, but the partner is only a symptom and mirror for the events that have hurt your soul with dark shadows long before him.

I certainly do not want to reduce your destiny, but what good is a partner to you who is "guilty"?

My experience of the last few decades is: Neither will this save your soul, nor will it diminish the true inner distress which has led to this fate.

How can love ever be experienced as complete when we had to split off the love for ourselves? How can we ever feel and really perceive another person as a whole when we had to distance ourselves from our own feelings in order to survive in an emotionless family and a cold, unfeeling environment? What can ever replace one's own feeling of being a person worthy of love?

Nothing cripples and alienates a soul as much as a trauma. The earlier in life it took place and the more often it happened, the more the feeling of powerlessness, external control and unhappy love is present in the life of an adult.

For those affected, their inner distress of is often in-
tangible and inexpressible and it is unbelievable for
anyone else who has not experienced this themselves.
Permanent overload with conscious and unconscious
thought loops, work or escape programmes often
leave little room for the joyous side of life. Only the
concrete and targeted processing of mental injuries
and resulting mental splits can lead traumatised people to new levels of personal freedom. This way a new
capacity for happiness can develop even for people
entangled in the deepest suffering.

Only when the origin of the unhappiness in your life is
understood and integrated, you will have a chance to
really feel whether the partner by your side is the right
one for your life.

With all the knowledge in this guide, the longing for a
complete love relationship can become the target of a
personal commitment to take the responsibility for your

own happiness into your own hands with new courage.

Before we finally leave this part now, I would like to use a concrete example to give you an idea of why traumatic experiences generally cannot be resolved with one or two sessions or a weekend course. The following outline is neither universally valid nor complete.

Let's take a closer look at the possible levels of a child which has been abused by a paedophile father for years:

1. Panic, fear, threat to life, betrayal

    - Inner withdrawal, leaving the body, dissociation
    - Trauma by first abuse experience

2. Panic, fear of next abuse

    - Trauma of the permanent threat to life
    - Escape, defence useless
    - Confusion, feelings of guilt
    - Escape into the "perfect world", fantasy family

3. Submission to the inevitable

    - Individual survival plan, survival strategy
    - Reclassification into something as good as possible
    - Development of parts loyal to the perpetrator

4. Starting puberty: fear, panic …
    … not to be "loved" anymore

- fear of loss (loss trauma)

... to be discarded (feelings of sudden worthlessness)

... not to be "useful" anymore (feelings of sudden uselessness)

... and the feeling that all the years of endurance have been in vain (rage & hopelessness)

... and the attempt to delay growing and growing-up (to remain a "child" for daddy)

... as well as escape and addiction – first escape experiments even into suicide (life escape)

5. Since "puberty" – after being "side-lined" – shift of the pent-up rage, fear, panic, for example to the body level

... in order to draw attention on oneself – "look", I feel so bad

... in order to distract oneself from the other things that had been happening for years

... silent protest to demand affection (there is no reward other than to survive)

... therefore often deep forgetting of the incomprehensible in order to be able to survive in a current state of dependency (parents / caregiver – child)

... through autoimmune diseases (rebellion in the body, self-destruction of what has no worth for others anymore)

6. As an adult: panic attacks, sudden panic, burn-out
... caused for example by divorce, separation, unemployment, death of mother or father (own family or the partner's family)

... and unconscious remembering of never really having had a mother or a father

Feelings of worthlessness, uselessness and failure
remind a part of us of something much worse, older,
forgotten. The escape from the trauma in childhood
becomes a "curse" for the adult who does not remember the trauma anymore.

If you imagine that the father has sold his child to other
"fellow sufferers" (e. g. colleagues) to top up his pocket
money and that is not the worst thing the child had to
experience, you can probably also imagine why I have
developed to become an expert in many areas and
continue researching this area together with others.
The processing of such complex psychological traumas needs time, patience and experience.

Each phase needs your awareness-forming, recognition, processing and your compassion.

Not all ways are easy. In my opinion, there is only one
worthwhile goal!

And what about the mother? In the adoration of the
mother children often sacrifice themselves to the father
in order to bring relief to the mother. In order to be able
to live with the father, a part of the child also has to
suppress, deny, forget the "sacrifice". This leads to
psychological splits which can become evident in
physical symptoms, different life phenomena and behaviour patterns in later life.

Those who are seriously searching for answers, as I do, will have to leave the addiction (work, games, drugs, sex, free time, holiday, sport ...) someday and maybe recognise the message someday – addiction = the search for your Trauma.

Or the person will pause someday in his flight (forward) and recognise –
Flight = fly before T = the real curse is the flight from the T = flight from the Trauma, the trauma which has been forgotten while you were fleeing towards the future

Why am I writing all this here?

As long as you are – consciously or unconsciously – fleeing from yourself and from the things you have experienced, you will never be able to enter into a love relationship completely. Even in a golden palace the most precious fruits will someday leave a stale taste. But perhaps all that is complete nonsense.

It might depend on the fruits and in the garden of another prince or princess there must surely be sweeter fruits. Or not?

What Could You Learn for Your Relationships from This Part?

From Part 5, I would like you to learn the following:

**If as a child
you have to learn
to forget,
you will have difficulties
remembering
as an adult.**

**We only notice
the limits
we live in
when we
try to change them.**

Trauma with all its consequences becomes a kind of "habit".

Since we have never known any different, we often do not question the manifestations, phenomena and life patterns intensively enough, or not at all.

The resolution and "re-adaptation" of life and relation-ship patterns resulting from trauma is always disturbed by learnt, habitual reflexes.

I have one more wish for you. If something has touched you on these last pages, take it seriously.

Checklist for Part 5 – What Exactly Can You Do Right Now?

Step 5

Clarifying Your Own Limits

When you start to formulate and to follow your own desires, which go beyond the boundaries of your current life parameters, you will notice the following: You run up against obstacles and in some areas against invisible borders which only make each of your efforts seem absurd. All formulae for success, decades of perseverance and your all-round talent do not seem to bear any fruit for you personally. You can probably help many other people but not yourself.

Perhaps you have even given up on some of your wishes, which you have hopefully noted down in Part 2, because of this.

When we encounter limits in our lives which cannot be overcome with hard work and talent alone for a long time, we sometimes cannot do anything other than to challenge the "guardians" of these limits, as I call them, to show themselves. They might already have shown themselves in your life but you did not understand the message or the connection. I hope this chapter has clarified a few things for you.

Behind the "guardians" of our life limits, blind spots often show up in our life history, family secrets and taboos. If we look deeper, we often come into contact with feelings and split-off parts of our personality caused by severe injuries in our earlier childhood. Change is only possible here if we admit to such limits and call them by their name. For example:

I have this particular sexual behaviour pattern and would like to understand and change it.
I have these characteristics of trauma and would like to understand and change them.

The second step is then to organise adequate support and advisors for yourself, since it is impossible to solve these issues by yourself. But before you learn in the next part what you should be especially aware of when doing so, I have a few particular questions. Please write down specific notes to spontaneous answers.

- Which part of your own life story do you remember?

- Which part of your story do you only know from other people's stories?

- Which part of your family history has never been talked about (taboo)?

- Which of the stories you were told cannot be true?

- Which questions have you never dared to ask?

- Do you know the true cause for your "bad luck" in your life, in your relationship?

- Which topics have you never dug deeper into – and have made do with the first answer you got?

- In relation to what topics do you consciously leave other people (child / partner) in the dark?

- Which answers are you so much afraid of that you prefer to take **M**edicine, **A**lcohol, **D**rugs?

- Which sexual behaviour patterns or characteristics of trauma mentioned in this chapter do you know from your own experience?

Freedom through Free Room

Remove possible trigger points from your home environment, ideally today. Those might for example include furniture, pictures or jewellery that create a conscious or unconscious connection to people who you associate traumatic events with. This recommendation stands even if you believe you have already completely processed your history.

The table that belonged to the grandmother who almost drowned you or your child will always remain the table that unconsciously reminds you of this event. The expensive bracelet that perhaps your husband has given you after he almost beat you to death will always reflect the connection to the perpetrator and your life-threatening experience. The family picture above the fireplace with its deceptively ideal world will be like a knife that every day injures you and the parts of you that have never seen this "ideal world". The house inherited from your parents will always remain a

238

place where you have been mistreated, humiliated, imprisoned or abused as a child.

Step by step, room by room, area by area, clear your living space and remove everything that creates a connection to the perpetrators in your life. Do not forget about the garage, the storage room or the basement. Give it away, sell it, pawn it or auction it off. You are entitled to this compensation.

You should however keep those things that will serve as proof and evidence of what really happened to you. You can and should store letters, photos, videos or diaries which help to reconstruct the truths about your personal life story all together in a place which you can call the place of truth. Maybe these steps will also help you to become aware of how bad it really was for you. If you touch this point, you might perhaps for the first time feel the desire to open up to someone who will listen to you and help you to reconquer your inner free space. You should trust and follow this feeling.

**There is another particular thing
you can and should do.**

Build Up Your Reserves of Vital Materials

Living with trauma is like top-level sport for your body and nervous system.

The only difference is that there is almost no recovery time because as mentioned before, trauma does not stop by itself. Stressful situations are accompanied by highly complex processes in the body which among other things need vitamins and minerals. Traumas rob your body of vital materials and therefore inevitably lead to a weakness of the whole immune system in the long-term, resulting in tiredness, exhaustion and lack of concentration.

It is not possible to create a vibrant relationship
in total exhaustion.

With or without a traumatic background, you should always take care of yourself and provide yourself with sufficient reserves of vital materials, ideally with a high quality nutritional supplement. Unfortunately there are only a few recommendable products on the global market. Having searched for adequate products for years, I have finally found a German producer whose products will certainly give you instant results as well. But check for yourself.

Better take vitamins
that produce effects
than medication
with side-effects!

02/02/2000

Follow this direct link to the producer's shop: http://www.vitamin-leben.com You can choose your language via the globe symbol. Not all products are available in all countries.

If you want to ensure
that your opposite gets your heart racing,

you best make sure
that it is well looked after.

Direct link to Q10 - http://www.Q10.vitamin-leben.de

I would like to particularly recommend you try the liquid **Q10** product here. I am sure it has saved my life. If you are interested, check your personal requirements. What works well for me is taking about 15-20 drops 2-3 times a day. In case of acute stress I take more. This "heart vitamin" is absorbed very quickly by the body. In cases of tachycardia, palpitations, "rumbles" or "stutters", the Q10 depot might simply empty. Those who are familiar with recurring nightmares or panic attacks tend to use up extremely high amounts of this body's own substance. Since the body's own Q10 production reduces from the age of around thirty, many people end up with an increasing "Q10 deficit". If you are carrying the additional burden of trauma, this may become life-threatening before you even notice. This advice does not replace any medical examination or the processing of backgrounds to personal stress. I used to have this "emergency treatment" by my bedside for over 10 years. I still always carry it in my handbag. Thanks to the processing of my own story with trauma constellation, the cardiac symptoms and nights filled with nightmares have become significantly less than before. Taking Q10 after nightmares has proved very useful.

Positive side effects:
1. The physical body experiences love and care and direct help where previously there was none.

2. You become active and help yourself. You break through earlier experiences of inability to act and establish a new, self-determined pattern of action.

I also find the daily support with a **B-vitamin complex (AOP)** very useful, which also serves as an energy source. This is because a further consequence of trauma is an increased requirement for vitamin B. To put it simply I could also say that traumas are real "vitamin B devourers". This is partly due to the many unconscious control and survival programmes that consume considerable resources. Just imagine you had to fight against powerful pressure to keep a large lid or door closed and at the same time manage your profession or retirement, family, sports and leisure activities, 24 hours a day, for decades. On a physical level, this internal pressure often manifests itself as high blood pressure. In emergencies, trust recommendations by the medical emergency personnel. I do however recommend that you consider trauma therapy as an additional measure in case of high blood pressure phenomena and "symptom cocktails" of all kinds.

The more medication you take, the more important additional highly effective vital substances and highly active, living water become for detoxification. If you are unsure whether you should take a certain drug or not, simply ask yourself whether you really want to have the possible side effects. When in doubt, choose products where the list of possible positive effects is significantly longer than that of the possible side-effects. Your body will be grateful to you.

Tried lots of different things - no success yet?

Direct link to AOP - http://www.1.vitamin-leben.de
– B-vitamin-complex
Please take a maximum of 1x dosage scoop, included
in the packaging. The rapid absorption by the body
may lead to an unexpected sensation of heat. This
may be felt in the head area and lead to redness in the
face. This short-lived, well known "flushing effect" does
not constitute an allergic reaction and is dependent on
the dosage used. 2-3 doses per day are a good
benchmark.

If something or someone catches your eye, it's
worth taking a closer look.
http://9.vitamin-leben.de – for relaxed looks

Interested in a delicious Power-Drink-Mix?
- 1x daily, before breakfast for example
Simply order using the following direct links:
- http://1.vitamin-leben.de- 1 scoop AOP
- http://2.vitamin-leben.de- 1 sachet basics
- http://3.vitamin-leben.de- 1 sachet fitness drink
- http://4.vitamin-leben.de- 18 drops Q10
-
fill everything in - http://7.vitamin-leben.de into a shak-
er, top up with 6-700ml still water or tap water, mix
contents and enjoy. I use activated, "living" water.

Power-Drink-Mix for two persons:
- http://1.vitamin-leben.de- 2 scoops AOP
- http://2.vitamin-leben.de- 2 sachets basics
- http://3.vitamin-leben.de- 1 sachets fitness drink
- http://4.vitamin-leben.de- 25 drops Q10

Evenings: http://5.vitamin-leben.de mix 2-3 measuring spoons in a glass

The following links regarding these recommendations are country specific:

Austria: Power-Drink
http://1AT.vb2.de http://2AT.vb2.de http://3AT.vb2.de
http://4AT.vb2.de http://7AT.vb2.de
Evenings: http://5AT.vb2.de   Eyes: http://9AT.vb2.de

Switzerland: Power-Drink
http://1CH.vb2.de http://2CH.vb2.de http://3CH.vb2.de
http://4CH.vb2.de http://7CH.vb2.de
Evenings: http://5CH.vb2.de   Eyes: http://9CH.vb2.de

International: Power-Drink
http://1EN.vb2.de http://2EN.vb2.de http://3EN.vb2.de
http://4EN.vb2.de
Evenings: http://5EN.vb2.de

Our cells need the best possible care every day. Healthy cells divide healthily. Cell renewal happens in phases of 90 days.

Do you want to try it out first?
In our practice we always have activated water available. You are welcome to speak to me about a power-drink-tasting in connection with an individual consultation or one of our seminar days.

Forever young? It's worth a try.

DE	EN
http://98.vitamin-leben.de	http://98EN.VB2.de
http://99.vitamin-leben.de	http://99EN.VB2.de
http://100.vitamin-leben.de	http://100EN.VB2.de

AT/Austria	CH/Switzerland
http://98AT.VB2.de	http://98CH.VB2.de
http://99AT.VB2.de	http://99CH.VB2.de
http://100AT.VB2.de	http://100CH.VB2.de

I always endeavour to keep links up to date. I do not have any influence over offers or changes to the shop by the manufacturer. Should the links no longer work, the quality of the products no longer meets my expectations or I can no longer provide the finance or technical support for this service. Therefore, don't delay; take advantage of the vital substance power right now. Your body will thank you for a life full of vital substances.

If these are issues that concern you, have you ever thought about your illness and questioned any long-term medication? Might there be new alternatives today?

There are many gates to freedom, the only question is which key fits.

03/06/2008

Part 6 Counselling Under the Microscope

Why Most Courses, Seminars, Therapies and Techniques Cannot Help You to Improve Your Life

Among other things, you will learn here why many advisors, therapists and types of therapies cannot help you and why possibly – particularly always in your case – nothing works at all. With this knowledge you will save a lot of time, nerves and above all stacks of money from now on.

If the journey
is the destination
it is no wonder
that life
falls by the wayside.

23/06/2010

If our happiness in love and life leaves much to be desired, it would seem reasonable that we should start to expand our knowledge. We gather new ideas and try to increase our success in life. We want to enjoy life before it is over. Lots of books, courses, seminars, therapies and techniques promise to help us. On my own journey through life I have tried out and got to know many of them.

Globally there are many wonderful instructors and seminar leaders who you can listen to with pleasure for days. There are so many creative training concepts and techniques which can really help you to feel somewhat better and sometimes even fantastic. But in my experience, this "kick" rarely has more value than a weekend with an interesting book, a fascinating movie or a rousing concert. You can save yourself a lot of time and money there! Why is that so?

As long as you cannot raise the anchor, even the most beautiful sails will not help you. Even if it feels fabulous to see the wind billowing in the sails.

In NLP, new "anchors" are even set in order to bring the life ship on course – an interesting allegory, isn't it? If that still does not help, you can "sweep away" everything that is disturbing with a "swipe". A brilliant idea. It sucks though if life is still stuck despite all the various beautiful new anchors.

"Yes, but …"! I hear the waves, I see the sails blowing in the wind and another ship on the horizon. I already taste the salt on my lips and I feel how the boat moves on the water. Surely I must be out on sea by now. Mustn't I? – Yesterday I saw an interesting movie. The most important key sentence in it is: "Don't forget to turn around". That helped a woman to notice the key to survival just in time, which was floating in the water behind her. She would have drowned otherwise, since she was tied to an anchor with chain and lock which drew her into the depths. The mystery thriller is called *Half Light*, Demi Moore plays the main part in it and the movie is at times not for the faint-hearted.

Why am I telling you this now?

With so many seminars, therapies and positive think-ing, many people lose their normal approach to life. They live more in fantasy than in reality. Turning around is not allowed. After all, you should look for-ward in life and not back.

Some people might find that they have not moved an inch. And then?

Then all the lovely success at the seminar would have been for nothing. Wouldn't it?

Have you often had the feeling that despite everything you have done so far the real problems of your soul have been never touched? Why is that so?

There is a huge difference between new life pro-grammes which you would like to install or have installed on "your system" and old, often traumatic ex-periences from childhood that stop them from functioning. Your new "desired programmes" (dream weight, dream partner, dream profession …) usually have to be reloaded and started from scratch again and again and then supplied with lots of energy (posi-tive thinking) to keep them going. A TRAUMA and programmes from childhood are there 24 hours / 7 days a week and are running constantly.

You do not even have to turn on the "PC" for that. You cannot change such "system programmes" by "playing around" with their programme interfaces.

See also the closing remarks at the end of the last chapter.

The most lucrative business in the world is probably the business with people's desire and hope that a beautiful new world can be created quickly and easily. A few beautiful success stories, some nice effects and already the eloquent seminar leader has his paying audience in his pocket. Only for you as a participant, the only really lasting effect is the hole in your wallet.

Do you still have the impression that there are obviously people who have positively changed their lives with this seminar / "amazeballs"/ XY...? And you are the only person did not manage to achieve their goal? Surely you did something wrong, did not understand something correctly or you do not believe profoundly enough in it. Or is it the lack of belief in the technique, method or your imaginary dream goals?

What does this feeling remind you of?

It is down to you – is it your own fault? Nobody really loves you? Nobody understands you? Do not go away. Please stay with this feeling of "misfortune", failure in your life. You are an adult now but with this strange feeling you always feel somehow helpless and small? How helpless? How small? Almost like a child? How old might this child be?

Ask the child what it has experienced – why it feels so helpless. Listen carefully to what it has to say. If you really mean it, you will gain its trust. It might take you some time. Also explain your own story to the child as far as you remember it. While doing so, stay in touch with your feelings and be honest.

Maybe you will remember bit by bit that you had already had this feeling as a child which still accompanies you even now that you are an adult. Panic? Despair? Sadness? The idea that it would have been better if you had never been born? The feeling that everything is always down to you and you alone? The fantasy that your childhood / your parents / your world could be much better if only you were different? But you cannot change anything about it? – What exactly is it you need to change?

Do you really believe that the child you were back then had a chance to find out how to change the world for itself?

The truth is:

Here, success strategists and "superficial thinkers" are completely out of their depth.

Helplessness and despair always have an origin. Prolonged helplessness and despair lead to a trauma. Perhaps this is the truth which explains why many seminar concepts and therapy techniques never work for you of all people. At least you are honest enough to admit the failure of these concepts. Take another step forward. Become the advocate for your soul.

And the others? Have you contacted them after 6, 12, 24 months? Go through your contacts and seminar address lists. Ask what other people can tell you about really lasting, positive changes in their lives a few months after the great seminar / XY / ....

The greatest benefit is usually meeting interesting people like you there. Such encounters often result in friendships lasting a lifetime.

Before we proceed to the practical part, we have to clear up one other frequently asked question. **Why do successful people who have everything they need so often decide to end their life?**

With good instructors and intensive coaching our survival Self can function at its highest performance for a long time. But a "sick soul" will not let itself be fobbed off with worldly successes in the long-term. This "old unhappiness" within us wants to be understood and appreciated. If nobody recognises this, the person's inner need becomes even greater, their life more and more senseless. The worldly consolation plasters cannot prevent the pus-filled wound bursting open anymore. In my opinion, the clearing up of mental injuries and splits should therefore be of utmost priority and should be accompanied by a healthy portion of positive thinking. Then even people like you and I will be able to see and enjoy long-term luck in both partnership and profession. For this, we do not need any illusionary ideal worlds or success fantasies. Successful people who end their lives show us: inner mental peace cannot be substituted by any amount of money in the world. However, the idea that the mental distress stops with the escape into suicide is merely a wide-spread illusion. My many years working with "lost souls" confirm that there is no doubt about that.

On the other hand there are many people who believe the illusion that everything will be better when they are finally "successful". No journey is too long, no seminar too expensive for them in order to achieve this. Some people need many years to finally realise that other people are no different from anybody else and that hardly anything that shines really is gold. Many business ideas specifically use psychological patterns here. The more elite the character, the greedier the customers. By all means treat yourself to such experiences and distractions if your pocket money amounts to four or five digit figures. Some offers provide truly fascinating entertainment. To all others I recommend not to clutch at golden straws and "instant solutions" of the "wish for anything" kind. Save your money. As a rule, you won't miss a thing. Do not blow your savings book money or your life insurance on other people's golden curtains and plates. Is that clear enough?

Just to be clear:
I am a fan of inspired further education and support by people from whom we can learn to better organise our professional and private environment. But it remains a life-long challenge to better understand and love ourselves in particular. Life is too short to find everything out on your own. Therefore, I always recommend a mix of motivation, inspiration and transformation. This guide is especially dedicated to the often neglected transformation of hindering, unclear influence structures.

The trick is to feel complete, authentic and happy with yourself, right now, in this moment. Then life does not fall by the wayside along the self-improvement journey in seminar and therapy rooms.

Point of Reference:
The success of the "flat taste" is the recognition of its true essence.
The idea of "positive thinking" has many friends among sufferers although this concept alone rarely provides them with long-lasting help.

TRAUMA can only be processed and cleared up by finding the truth, not a new illusion.
Early childhood experiences with traumatic consequences have more of an impact than attending 100 success or angel seminars.

Suicide often shows the failure of a survival strategy which is fleeing from the clarification of deeper mental injuries, responsibility and truth.

Positive thinking is a successful survival strategy. However, it only resembles the "carrot" for the mule and the "wind" for the sails. In order to really lift the "anchor" you might have to do something else.

PS: Not all life problems have their origin in a trauma.

But if you fail to see any success after more than two success seminars and strict application of their recommendations, a weekend visit with trauma constellation will definitely widen your horizon in a useful way.

Do not let yourself be misled any longer, pick up the reins yourself!

What Could You Learn for Your Relationships from This Part?

From Part 6, I would like you to learn the following:

- There are areas and issues in relationships which cannot be changed with understanding and patience alone.

- Trauma structures do not dissolve by themselves even in unconditional love.

- As a partner you can and should not try to substitute a therapist.

- If couples therapy has "failed", it primarily means that the form of therapy was not the right one for the issue or you as a couple, assuming there is a real common interest in clearing up issues and finding solutions.

- The blindness for trauma is commonplace among doctors, advisors, mediums, therapists and other persons who earn money with counselling services.

- The processing of trauma requires courage, perseverance and professional help.

Karmic relationships are similar to some criminal cases. Some of them can only be fully resolved decades later. In criminology, the DNA test has already revealed many truths. For me this is comparable with the discovery of trauma and its consequences lasting for many generations.

Thanks to the discovery by Prof Dr Franz Ruppert there is the possibility to make traumatic events and imprints visible in three-dimensional form and to process them by using the method of constellation of the intention, thus clearing up causes and backgrounds of unhappy love relationships and all phenomena in relationships and life stories which thus far have been marred by lovesickness, pain of separation and endless nagging questions.

Perhaps you have been disappointed and frustrated to such an extent over the years that you have decided never to visit a seminar or trust a therapist again. After all the things which I have experienced myself I can understand that very well. I am well acquainted with utter despair, helplessness and an attitude of giving up. If you still have hope despite everything you experienced with advisors and are searching for alternatives or a recommendation then I would like to point you in the direction of multi-generational psycho-traumatology according to Prof Dr Franz Ruppert.

I am certain that you will also find a good individual solution and answer in trauma constellation using the constellation of your personal intention. This method is based on the bonding and trauma theory. Its aim is the integration of your own split parts of personality and the dissolution of unhealthy symbiotic entanglements. This path will guide you through your life and step by step lead you out of your own illusions or illusions which you took over into healthy autonomy, real love, mental and emotional clarity. If you can identify with this book, this process-orientated work is bound to be able to help you. I have been specialising in this myself since 2009.

Special Features and Possibilities of Trauma Constellation

- Recognition and release from entanglements with foreign feelings

- Recognition and release from entanglements with trauma taken on from someone else

- Recognition, processing and dissolution of perpetrator-victim-splits

- Encounter with and integration of split personality fragments

- Clearing up of life patterns, self-destructive and sabotage mechanisms

- Clearing up of life questions, phenomena and physical symptoms of all kinds

Checklist for Part 6 – What Exactly Can You Do Right Now?

Step 6

Clarification on Suitable Counsellors

If you come up against limits in your life and your relationship which you would like to change and notice that you simply can't manage it, it is a good time to search for suitable help and advice.

The following questions might help you with that:

- Do you trust this person spontaneously or can you build up trust?

- Is this person trained in trauma therapy?

- Is the doctor trained to recognise the link between possible physical symptoms and trauma – if you are searching for / need the help of a doctor?

- Are you sure you aren't just being offered imaginative procedures?

- Is your advisor afraid of topics such as trauma, sexuality, abuse or ritual violence?

- Do you have the feeling that you can really talk about everything?

- Do you have the feeling that they believe everything you tell them?

- What is the deepest pain inside you? How would you describe your intention and issue which you would like to change?

- What would be a first good step in this direction for you?

- Are you really ready to change those limits for your "dream state" of partnership which have been determined by your life story?

In the following part you will find guidance and exercises which you can immediately put to use for yourself and your relationships!

**Experience
is the consequence
of a willingness
to act.**

21/11/2010

Part 7: Aids to Orientation and Exercises

A Partner like My Father / My Mother

Who hasn't heard about it or experienced it themselves? Have you ever really understood it?

If you feel like you have married your mother / your father but this has not made you feel like you're on "cloud nine", you are encountering an unsolved conflict from your childhood in your partner.

If this is the case, it wasn't your healthy adult part that chose the partner but a childhood part inside you that had to idealise the father / the mother in order to survive and is still living in this fantasy world today.

Where the embryo, infant or child is directly or indirectly confronted with mental cruelty, violence and abuse, these experiences must be explained, split off and suppressed in the child's world of innocent love. This is the only way to survive. At this stage the child creates ideal fantasy worlds in which the parents are very different.

In the child's struggle to survive against the hard reality in an unbearable, life-threatening home, the "caregivers" are often converted to foster parents and the "real parents" to people who died early or were lost.

Because this concept of an ideal world works so well in terms of survival, many adults are mystified if they encounter a partner who drinks, is violent, controlling, dominating and jealous. The cruel reality of a suppressed childhood literally strikes especially women particularly hard. Unfortunately, this "strike" does not usually serve as a wake-up call. On the contrary. It reactivates the conditioned, childish survival mechanism to explain everything in love, to understand the perpetrator and even to defend him to others. Here, friends who want to help are very often not appreciated because they present a threat to the ideal world fantasy. In such cases you can really only be of help to someone if you acknowledge the childish protection mechanism (which has to deny reality in order to survive). If "this child" feels itself noticed, you have a chance to convey the bigger picture to the adult to show them the possibilities of a new freedom.

If this has given you goosebumps you also will understand why you will never be able to change your partner and will never come to a solution or a change directly through them.

People with problematic childhoods have to blank out and redefine parts of reality in order to survive. With this in mind it is no wonder if your siblings or friends later notice how similar the partner is to the father / mother – often also in their looks. As long as people still live in their ideal world repression they themselves are often blind to obvious connections.

In choosing a partner, another aspect plays a crucial role as well.

Since we were not able to do this as a child, as adults we still try to meet the idealised father / mother in the partner in order to finally be able to feel the parental love which the child always had to forego despite all its longing. These programmes function on a completely unconscious level and therefore they can only be understood, stopped and changed with great awareness and clarity. An important step in this context is the recognition of the childhood as it really was.

If you are ready to exchange all illusions and ideal world fantasies for the truth about your "lost childhood", you will be able to recapture a healthy ability to love for the adult inside you and thus create the opportunity for a new dimension in partnership. This partnership will be able to function beyond the longing for daddy or mommy and be free of the "hard realities" which you may have had to deny as a child.

Note:
If you know and acknowledge
your childhood
as it really was,
you will be able to see your partner
as he / she really is.

Better off Without a Partner?

Sexuality and Damnation – the Karmic Relationship with Life

An organism which was created by sexuality will, consciously or unconsciously, always feel attracted by energies of carnal desire and sexual ecstasy. The more the type of the encounter corresponds to one's own desires, imaginations or prohibitions, the stronger the attraction. Only children have no choice in this context. They are shaped by influences which are determined by their closest caregivers. If intensive psychological splits take place here, it may also be that sexuality itself is seen as the source of all evil and therefore split off. It basically disappears from life, like some people in caves, hermitages or monasteries. There, the experience with sexuality suppressed and split off in childhood often repeats itself later as it was before – in secret. Or despite years of "mediation", these people do not find the inner freedom they are searching for, or the desired "enlightenment".

Longing for sexuality and the joy of it is a natural need which people should follow in a healthy way to an old age.

The natural exchange of closeness, tenderness and sexuality helps to support the body's vitality. Therefore, singletons should find pleasant opportunities for themselves, without the feeling of shame, in order to enjoy the pleasure of their own sexuality and sensuality. And maybe also in order to gain helpful, new experiences. Here it is important to find a nice way which opens a natural integration into everyday life and which is not so much burdened by the taboo of something forbidden.

Society still has a way to go in developing mindfulness and appreciation regarding this topic as well. Part of this will also be to shed much more light on and bring to attention topics such as abuse, incest and mal-treatment in the family, since it is here that real dangers lie for society as well.

Should you have banished sexuality to the "hell of damnation" – and all people who can enjoy it too –, I wholeheartedly recommend that you research these signs of psychological injury down to their origin. I know you probably don't want to hear it but people who live their lives resisting against or completely cut-ting out tenderness and sexuality have as a rule been massively traumatised in their life by this issue. There is good news – today there are possibilities to regain the innate freedom and to enjoy the natural happiness of life with a fulfilled sexuality without shame.

Through the processing of your burdensome history you will gradually feel the freedom grow inside you to choose to a new form of life. One day, you will feel amply rewarded by it. Now I do not want to hear any-thing about age. Just forget about it. As long as you can breathe, you can act!

And tenderness of any kind is a very healthy "pastime" even at the age of 120.

Even if so far you only know sexuality from books or films. Even in your life there is a vibrant place for your own joyful experience with it. If you find the courage to look the truth of your life story in the face, you will choose people and a place where you are met in suitable mindfulness, appreciation and professionality. If necessary, ask people you trust to accompany you while taking your first steps (counselling, seminar, therapy) into an unknown area.

There are people like me who will never make fun of you.

Therefore I can only assure you: You are welcome at any age!

By the way: We are talking about your karmic relationship with life itself here and about your perhaps still unconscious and unspoken complaint that this life still owes you something.

You are a definite part of the decision on how the topic of sexuality evolves in our society. It is your personal "shadow" over which you may jump in order to change something positively. If you have cleared up and understood your karmic relationship with life you will also discover new joys in other relationships in life.

You are an important part of our society and others who want to live in joy beyond the "damnation" will be happy to follow you.

Every one of us carries the responsibility for how long divine freedom and humanity will be trampled on for. If there is a life after death for you and a next life here on Earth, it can only become better if you are ready now to bring your fate into light.

Life itself is, like this guide, just the seed. You can only harvest the fruits you may be waiting for if you are ready to accept the challenge again and again which this seed is carrying in itself.

Sex or Love?

Admittedly a provocative title. Everyone has different ideas about love and sexuality. Often these are influenced by our parents, the media or historical developments, without us even being aware of it. In order to ensure cultural survival after wars or disasters in history, sometimes sex for the purpose of procreation was more important than love. Where only a few men survived, they were sometimes responsible for providing numerous offspring. It wasn't unusual for several women to share a man and consider this to be a normal thing, depending on the circumstances. Regardless of such historical characteristics and reproaches by the two genders that while one ascribes far too much or not enough importance to "love", "sexuality" is far too important or not important enough for the other, I would like to consider principal influences on possible experiences with sex and love. Once again it is important to me here to give all those food for thought whose lives continually give rise to questions regarding this topic.

Do you also know the phenomenon of being able to experience a very fulfilling, joyful, sexual relationship in partnerships or a level of great genuine love? To experience both together does not seem to be possible in your life or became another mystery in your history after a short exemplary experience?

Sensuality and eroticism in conjunction with unconditional love definitely come together much more rarely in love relationships than people would wish. If this is an issue you find yourself dealing with then you will find information about important correlations and a possible answer here.

When people feel that they have to choose between "money and love" or "sex and love" they often end up in deep emotional conflicts. The incompatibility of these tiers is the subject of many novels and films.

Life stories – maybe yours, too – are therefore often characterised by decades of extreme contradiction and tensions.

What would you choose now? Would you choose "love or money" – "love or sex"?

Do you know what sort of experiences and influences your decision is based on?

Do you know how to change the "or" into an "and"?

Truly helpful answers and explanations regarding this topic are very rare.

Due to a lack of alternatives, many solutions in life are determined by compromises and decisions that are most likely to enable you to carry on living. Since a "complete" love relationship does not seem to be possible, love affairs of all kinds, infidelities, double lives in partnerships, frequent changes of partners or long-term abstinence are widespread patterns in life whose individual merits are idealised by each person in their own way. The whole thing does however remain a puzzle game without a frame.

For people who are naturally faithful and romantic the challenge is just as great. What can you do when you feel that certain aspects in a relationship such as money, sex, love or health are missing, incomplete or "sick"?

What can you do when the man / woman is not able to achieve a "healthy mix" in the relationship?

Clear denial and abandonment of our own dreams and longings will eventually become an unloved part of our Self which we suppress and seldom put into question anymore. Quite a few people withdraw from society and from these tension creating aspects completely in order to find their "peace". Monasteries, ashrams, hermitages, larger living communities and caves are places people flock to worldwide. Every community that excludes one or more of those tension creating aspects inevitably becomes a magnet for people who find neither appropriate help nor answers in "normal" society. The only question is: Do you have to relinquish your money, your libido, your faith, your independence, your friends or a mixture of all of these at the entrance?

We can only achieve relaxation when tension creating aspects such as work can be removed (e. g. by going on holiday) or if the cause of these tension aspects is understood. However, the above-mentioned forms of community are often just vanishing points, offering only one answer which more often than not involves giving something up. For a short time, reflection and salutary reorientation is possible here, just like on holiday. In the long-term, unfortunately, the result is often self-sacrifice instead of a new self-understanding. My idea of a fulfilled life is very different. Those who stay in such communities for a long time often convince themselves that they have found the answer in abstention. This is often nothing more than a lack of courage to take on the responsibility for fulfilling one's own life dreams or the escape from an unknown truth. What truth? Do you really want to find out?

Point of Reference:
In any aspect of life
from which you separate yourself
for not being able to integrate it,
you only increase the chasm of a split
that already exists.

This increases your separation from yourself without understanding the underlying split. Every lover alongside another partnership / marriage indicates such a split. As described in Part 5, a split is the main feature denoting TRAUMA! In keeping with to our topic, constructive questions might for example be:

- What in your life caused the split between sex and love?

- Why is the sexual encounter in your partnership not as natural and joyful as the deep love between you would suggest?

<u>A specific example and a possible answer:</u>

Sexual abuse of children by parents or close contacts is incompatible with love, for it is life-threatening and anything but love. In order to survive, a child must be able to love the parents or close contacts unconditionally. Without realising what sexuality actually is, a child who has experienced or witnessed abuse must therefore separate this part from its own love. This results in a split. For an adult who has experienced something like this as a child – but does not remember – fulfilled sexuality with genuine love in a partnership usually remains unattainable because he/she had to realise their incompatibility very early on in order to survive.

It is therefore not surprising that phases in life where fulfilled sexuality and genuine heart-felt love seem to come closer together for these people are accompanied by life-threatening circumstances or cause life-threatening situations and frightening feelings.

If at the same time as we encounter the aspects that earlier led to a psychological split, our TRAUMA is triggered. We are confronted with all the feelings that were associated with it at that time. Sometimes we feel downright overwhelmed by panic, fear of death and other things without really knowing why. Therefore, the aspects associated with trauma (sex, love, tenderness...) can often only be experienced separately and at a distance – without the feeling of danger – by the affected persons until they have been processed and clarified. **Love-triangles can be a consequence.** You feel profoundly connected to one partner in deep love – sexuality is hardly significant here. With the other partner, sexual fulfilment is possible with deep devotion in a sensual, erotic relationship.

In one partnership, we may perhaps be in touch with our own capability for unconditional love from our childhood which was free from our own sexual needs – but was influenced by the sexual desire of others. In

275

other relationships we might be able to experience all the power of sexual ecstasy in complete surrender which we can enjoy and preserve only if we forego the love.

In the early childhood split, our own ability to love is saved and the pure innocent energy of sensual erotic joy is isolated in the act of human sexuality.

It is therefore not particularly helpful to condemn people rashly who have found their way of being able to experience important needs with the "model" of partnership and lovers. They thus preserve the distance between "sex" and "love" which is seemingly necessary for them without having to forgo one of these aspects completely.

Anyone who exerts "pressure" and wants to change something by "force" is bound to lose.

If for example someone in a sensual, erotic relationship also wants to talk about love in order to share this with the partner, they often unknowingly increase the pressure on traumatised parts of their personality. These personality parts will do anything to prevent the connection of the "critical factors". From experience, separation is the least of the evils for those parts. Especially if you have experienced this in your most exceptional relationship so far, you can be sure that there is very strong trauma in your and your partner's life story. In order to better understand these protective mechanisms, it is helpful to take a closer look at the topic of trauma. At the end of this book you will find selected recommendations.

The mental confusion caused by such traumas has almost incalculable, lifelong consequences. The uneasy feeling that something terrible will happen if you take the next step with the partner (moving together, engagement, marriage, children ...) often pushes responsible people to separation for example. Although on the one hand this "protects" the partner, it also results in two unhappy people who understand the secrets of partnerships even less than before.

It is as if the split in early childhood leads to the creation of two parts of the same polarity, which – similar to magnets with the same polarity – cannot approach each other at will. People who are exposed to such forces as adults increasingly feel disconnected from life itself, since it seems to hold more questions than answers and bring more suffering than joy of life for them. Further mental splits and withdrawal are the inevitable consequence.

In order to find clarity and peace, affected people often seek distance to all the contradictory and confusing feelings in life. In order to find a new direction and to survive, they seek refuge in a community outside conventional society.

There are many different forms of communities that consciously appeal to people in mental crises. Some are very good at using the people who come to them for their own purposes, without these people in need of help noticing what is actually going on. As a rule, the answer of vanishing point communities for people in life-crises is usually limited to the abstention from and exclusion of natural aspects of tension in life. Life there is rarely a path to personal freedom, independence and vitality. Daily life is often characterised by prohibitions, repression, dependency, abstention, exclusion (e. g. of public) and worship of "XY". Have you had your own experiences with this? You might also have only taken spiritual refuge to such a community or created your own "perfect world". What is your vanishing point strategy?

With this guide, I would like to invite you to embrace life once again with new answers. Use this knowledge actively to leave old dependencies and vanishing points. Make a conscious, new decision in favour of life with all its gifts.

Or would you prefer to remain in celibacy and depend on abstinence all your life?

Would you rather give all your money to an organisation / community and depend on not having any possessions for the rest of your life?

Or would you prefer non-committal group sex to paving the way for a sensual erotic partnership in unconditional genuine love?

I have nothing against your religion but would you really rather worship a God or guru instead of being a living example for a credible fulfilled life yourself?

Would you rather die at a "vanishing point" without really having tried everything to save your life, your dreams, your longings? Are you really sure that the salvation of your soul can be found at the "altar" that you may have chosen in your distress?

What answers did you get, assimilate from others or give to yourself?

Check for yourself with reference to the following table.

Tension aspects	Answers by vanishing point communities	Answer by BeSuCa
Sex	- Abstinence /voluntary celibacy or - Changing sex partners and group sex as "therapy"	- Recognising, understanding and solving of tension aspects - Trauma processing - Fullfilled, joyful sexuality in a steady relationship - "Quality" instead of quantity
Money	- Abstinence - Life for the community - Money to the community	- Financial self-determination by inspiration, motivation, creativity, vision & reality awareness
Love	- Abstinence from personal love affairs – Everyone loves only one person (adoration/god) or everyone loves everyone (also sexually)	- Ways to one´s own genuine love as a basis for a happy love affair

Result/ goal	– Pseudo freedom
	- Suppression, abstinence, separation
	– Splitting, ostracism, exclusion
	– Unreal world, illusion
	– Pseudo connection to vanishing points
	– Worship, glorification of gods and gurus
	– Giving up personal autonomy
	– Sometimes reflection, reversal, emotional strengthening
	– Separation, excess, perversion, disfigurement
	– Shifting aside of what causes the problems, handing over of own life responsibility
		– Truth, inner freedom
		– Spiritual clarity
		– Clearing up and integration of problems & life questions
		– Unconditional love for oneself and other worthy persons
		– Real feelings
		– New bonding capacity
		– Healthy autonomy
		  - one´s own opinion
		  - decision-making capacity
		– Clearing up and integration of what causes the problems, in self-responsibility

"Gates to Freedom" is a project that has arisen from such needs in order to reveal alternative paths that lead to a healthy autonomy beyond vanishing point communities.

The focus here is always on our own responsibility for our "divine freedom".

If this resonates with you, it would be my pleasure to accompany you along the way.

Point of Reference:
If you feel that there are certain things you can never experience together in your life (love, sex, money, health) although you desire it for yourself with all your heart and do your best to achieve it, you are probably getting a reference to an old mental split, possibly from early childhood, in connection with the elements which today seem to be mutually exclusive.
Incidentally, this applies likewise to all other issues in life that principally do not exclude each other.

Faith

For me, faith is
a direct personal experience.
To have faith, I do not need to become
a customer in a "company"
which makes faith its business.

Sex without Arousal

This is not about having to "perform" for your partner!

This is about one's own sexual self-liberation and the blissful experience of enjoying sexual ecstasy.

Sexuality is always an exchange and interaction between two partners. Since sex without arousal can only be one sided or does not take place at all, I would like to address another phenomenon in connection with sexuality here. I refer to it as "turning off of the sexual centre".

I mean the phenomenon of lack of arousal, lack of sensation or even numbness in the genital area. You may know this as "not being completely there" or you might call it "not being fully present". In men it is clearly visible to the partner and commonly referred to it as erectile dysfunction. The penis does not get hard at all or only with a lot of time and effort. In women this is a little more difficult to recognise. Generally the vagina remains dry or dries spontaneously. For a partner who enjoys caresses this does not go unnoticed, even if he uses a condom for contraception. For the women themselves this is often "normal", as they may not even know themselves any other way.

Note: These are all crucial moments of particular importance!

Such phenomena often appear more openly the greater the confidence or the love between the partners is.

You may have not have noticed this – in your previous relationships – or only in a very mild form.

Notwithstanding any medical conditions or lack of vital substances in the body, there can be the following underlying reasons:

- Overexcitement and uncertainty in the first night spent together

- Irritation and inconceivability by the surprisingly strong attractiveness of the other leads to a kind of "knock-out" – the nakedness of the other as a great gift (Am I awake or am I dreaming?) – Self-doubt – am I worth it – massively deflect sexual energy. The sooner and more frankly these things are discussed, the faster possible misunderstandings such as "I am probably not attractive enough" will be cleared up.

- complete exhaustion, fatigue, burnout, being overworked, stress

- wrong place / date, time pressure, disruptive general conditions

I personally also know the "turning off of the sexual centre" as an unconscious physical reaction during an encounter with a woman who has experienced deep emotional injuries at the hands of at least one another man. Sensitive people in particular often feel things about their partners which are not conscious to them or which they have forgotten. When a man or a woman has been emotionally massively injured and trauma-

284

tised by sexual abuse or otherwise, this drama is stored in the energy body. In the face of such wounds, our "sixth sense" often sends us a message via our bodies but we usually do not immediately understand such signs.

Perhaps as a woman you can give yourself to the man completely as long as he does not enter you. Your "shutdown" or "distancing yourself" occurs only in direct contact with the partner's penis.

Perhaps as a man you are strongly aroused when you look at your naked partner from a distance – but the closer you get to her, the more the arousal subsides.

Some people also need the caring help of the partner to notice that they "beam themselves away" completely while having sex. They probably had to learn this at some point in order to survive.

The phenomena here are very diverse and individual. The situation becomes particularly complex when both partners are affected by sexual and mental abuse or have been traumatised in other ways. In such cases, great honesty, perseverance and love are needed in a relationship. Such often confusing correlations cannot be figured out during a "one night stand".

I would therefore like to encourage you to take your feelings and physical reactions seriously and to talk to your partner about them very openly. This is mainly about awareness and appreciation, not about blame or accusations. At this point it is not necessary for you to know yet what possible causes might be at the heart of the problem. To find that out is another step.

In chapter "Karmic Relationships and TRAUMA" you can find many ideas and possible connections. Be glad that such phenomena shed light on hidden issues. Take advantage of the opportunity to appreciate old injuries in all mindfulness with your partner. Be gentle with yourself and your partner. Take the necessary time to develop a wholesome form of sexuality together in which all senses and physical areas may remain turned on. You will be rewarded with the feeling of a new sensuality and joy of life that provides every cell in your body with energy during sex. If you clear up your personal history you will definitely be able to markedly enhance your joint enjoyment of sexual encounters. Your love and mutual trust are important keys here. Sexuality in its most beautiful form is like a bath in pure life energy.

For some people sex does not work without love and they find it hard to admit this to themselves and to other people. Perhaps you are just not sure because the love you feel is so very different from usual or you do not know yet what "real love" feels like for you. Just enjoy the experience should it be like this someday. Thank yourself for having the courage to get to know yourself better. Thank your partner for the opportunity to have a close, human, perhaps intimate encounter. Always take the chance to feel and to show yourself completely authentic and honest.

A part of you may wish to "merge" with the other as quickly as possible, another part may want to take it slow and puts on the "brake". Perhaps you both feel that the relationship could become serious and neither of you wants to do anything wrong.

Point of Reference:

Talk openly about your contradictory or unsorted feelings. You can never lose anything this way that would have lasted. If you stay honest and authentic, a mindful encounter will never have an embarrassing ending. Thank everyone for the opportunity to find out who you really are.

The atmosphere in which a sexual encounter takes place always plays a crucial role of course. Not everyone can completely relax in the "closet". How much time had the couple spent together before? How long had they not seen each other? Since this is always an interplay between the partners, you will experience this differently in every couple constellation. The more you respect the individual energies in a partnership encounter and go with the "flow" without judging it, the faster you will open the space where your sexual encounter finds its most beautiful form. Allow yourself to rediscover your partner again and again and to get them back with tenderness when you realise that they are not completely there.

Point of Reference:
"Sex without Arousal" can reveal old emotional wounds in a trusting, attentive encounter and deep love. The mutual willingness to appreciate this reveals the special quality and challenge of a partnership.

Sexual self-liberation is often achieved by clearing up one's own mental injuries in connection to sexuality.

Sexual ecstasy derives from complete abandonment to the enjoyment of pleasure, pure sensuality and sexuality. In mindful attention to each other both partners find and create the context in which joyous sexuality can develop in complete presence.

Those who reveal their honest and authentic feelings will never lose anything that would have been lasting.

Eroticism

**is the encounter
of two gods
who give each other the most beautiful fruits
during the game of life.**

In our society, sexuality has been moving on a new level for some time. Both women and men therefore increasingly ask questions about changing experiences with sexuality. For those interested, answers are available on the DOUBLE AUDIO CD: *The new dimension of sexuality* - The recording is from my past as a "channel medium". It is still relevant today.

In a trusting encounter, the ability to let yourself go completely grows with the willingness to allow your own feelings to run freely even in a more intimate encounter. Sexual ecstasy thus becomes like a gift of divine joy to yourself.

Anyone who has experienced loss of control as life-threatening in a sexual situation then goes on to try to monitor any further sexual encounter as much as they can. This is mostly unconscious and prevents a full commitment to the possibilities of a new experience. This is comparable to you being responsible for security at a private party whilst at the same time trying to enjoy the party as a host.

Only once the previous events have been processed will it be possible to gradually develop a new "Yes" toward life and the experience of joyful sexuality. How would that feel? For a woman perhaps something like this:

Yes

A gentle tingling
rushed through my body –
I let myself fall
into the soft caress
which has just been
bestowed upon me
in a familiar way.

Every touch
seemed a gift to him,
every kiss
an adventure
which I was ready to embark upon with him.

My body seemed
to rise up towards him
as if freed from a thousand bonds,
like a spark
becoming light.

I felt nothing but the part
touched by his lips
like a royal fruit.

My thoughts
melted with his tongue
and I enjoyed the feel
of them following each other.
Yes.

18/09/2005

Escape from the Threatened Sexual Role

The development of a person's sexuality is massively influenced by their experiences in early childhood. If gender-specific characteristics lead to a threatening experience in childhood it may be an unconscious natural protective measure to deny these threatened usually sexual attributes.

The inner denial of threatened attributes of one's own physical appearance can cause a decrease of all gender-specific functions in their physical expression as well. The further development of one's own sexuality is delayed and "covered up" as far as possible in order to prevent the threatening experiences from becoming worse. This is of course only one possible reaction pattern as an example.

A girl who has been raped might start her monthly periods later than usual and forever experience them as very painful. The development of breasts may be delayed and rescinded to such an extent that they do not disturb the protection zone of "sexual neutrality". Even during a later pregnancy, the growing child will be "hidden" in such a way that it can hardly be noticed until delivery.

Direct breastfeeding of her own baby is not possible because of low milk production or severe pain. The desexualised, anonymous, mechanical suction process using a breast pump therefore works much better for affected women and is also less stressful.

An escape started in childhood from the threatened sexual role into an inconspicuous, neutral appearance takes place in the child's hope to avoid a further threat (abuse) or to limit the threat in the long-term at least. You can observe this survival strategy very clearly in some adult women's outer appearance and personal lifestyle. They only use female accessories sparingly, if at all. Jewellery, clothing and footwear send more neutral, unisex messages than sensually erotic, distinctly female signals. Here, conflicting feelings lead to many mixed forms of staying hidden on the one hand and on the other hand wanting to reveal oneself to the right partner nonetheless.

Often the distortion of one's own sexual role is perfected beyond recognition. You are bound to have also come across people who you were not able to classify clearly as either woman or a man, even at a second glance.

The most extreme form of fleeing from one's own damaged sexual role is expressed in gender reassignment. Here, we can see the escape into a new, undamaged, opposite-sex role. This is of course connected to the hope of being able to preserve the undamaged state of the new sexual identity. If the sexual influences from early childhood are not understood and processed, there is however a significant danger that such a person will attract the experience of life-threatening and abusive situations in their new sexual identity as well.

Men who have experienced sexual abuse may also unconsciously seek refuge in the denial of their own sexual male potency. Impotence can thus sometimes also be a physical protection method to ensure that the abused person never becomes like the man who committed the sexual abuse. The closer a male victim of sexual abuse comes to the age the former perpetrator was at the time, the stronger the protection mechanism becomes in such a case and the sexual ability (potency) to become a perpetrator is throttled.

Whatever an "escape or protection program" may look like – the longing for the unlived, natural, personal sensual and erotic part is always present. The liberation of this force and the expression of our own sexuality in a healthy, natural beauty can only be achieved by ourselves. A partner cannot accomplish this. In a loving relationship you can however receive great support and understanding for your process of sexual self-discovery.

Murder and Manslaughter – About the Success of Survival

Murder and manslaughter cannot only be found in books, films and on the street. It happens more often than many people might assume, even within one's own family.

Even today, many people are still affected by the effects of murder and manslaughter in earlier family generations. The more your ancestors were involved with these issues, the more likely it is that you might still be affected. The less honestly the topic is talked about, the less clear the family heritage is for offspring like you.

Unclarified, covered up murder and attempted murder often result in repetitions in subsequent generations. In relationships something like this may be perceived as a physically tangible threat with an unclear origin. This can manifest itself so strongly that you become worried that something might happen to your partner if you do nothing, but you feel helplessly exposed to this "ghost perpetrator". The only thing you can do is to end the relationship before it is too late. You might also try, consciously or unconsciously, to attract the "ghost perpetrator" to yourself to protect the partner. Without special knowledge many effects lead neither to the cause nor to the dissolution of the phenomena.

A special part of relationships is built on mutual longings, goals and future plans. The achievement of goals is known as "success" in the western world.

Despite their greatest efforts, for some people and couples this success seems to be unattainable. Are you committed beyond all measure, creative, helpful, likeable, friendly, highly qualified and deeply appreciated by others? Are you nonetheless unable to realise many goals – including partnership goals – due to the absence of professional and financial success?

Do you know these characteristics and phenomena in your life?

- a life like concrete

- massive and seemingly mysterious barriers to success

- living with "the handbrake on"

- any achievement of goals is only possible at a snail's pace

- nightmares

- precarious love relationships

If you are affected by this, I would like to provide you with information here as a suggestion for possible backgrounds. Perhaps you will be able to reveal your "secret" this way.

Any form of violence with unknown consequences and all thoughts of murder by people in our nearby environment affect our wellbeing and our development. Especially when we are very young.

Children whose parents or siblings have tried to kill them henceforth no longer feel that their lives are safe. Perhaps the mother had "poked about" with knitting needles as early as during pregnancy or had intentionally fallen down the stairs to cause a miscarriage, an abortion. Some women also jump off the table and try it that way.

Perhaps father or mother tried to smother the child in the crib or to poison it with food. Admittedly not a nice thought but unfortunately often a part of our reality. There are countless variations. It may also be that many ideas had "only" been played out in the thoughts of close caregivers. In any case, for us as children such a "climate" is life-threatening to the highest degree. It is unsafe, scary and dangerous 24 hours a day. To experience the parents or close caregivers (grandma, grandpa ...) as a threat is a shock and traumatic. Later, as adults, we often find it hard to build a trusting relationship with a person of the same gender as the one we perceived as the biggest threat to us in childhood.

Later we also often meet our own partner with this unconscious mistrust without being aware of what we are actually doing. Some of the implications of such childhood experiences are unimaginable. People affected by this may easily despair because of it as adults.

I hope attempted murder is not part of your biography. I do however know from my own experience how important it can be to recognise any indicators of such experiences in childhood. It will help you to understand a very special "secret of success".

Even if you experienced or witnessed a murder / attempted murder as a child, this can cause seemingly mysterious consequences on multiple levels of life in later years. What's the connection?

The same force which can be used to create something can also be used to destroy it. Anyone who has cut off all contact to the force that can destroy something in order to never become like ... will therefore have difficulties in work and careers as an adult to build something up that also brings real financial joy.

Why does this have such effect and particularly in these areas?

If you as a child felt that your life was under threat by active impulses on your father's or your mother's part, you could probably only survive your growing up in this "climate" by inwardly distancing yourself from that acting force.

Since you are, figuratively speaking, hiding the "knife" with which someone wanted to cut your throat, you will later find that you are missing the "tool" to "butter your bread" with.

In order to overcome persistent barriers to success that cannot be explained by a lack of qualifications or application, loving integration of targeted action impulses which have been split in traumas from early childhood is sometimes needed.

What would have happened to you as a child, if such a life-threatening impulse to act against you had really been "**successful**"?

What if your father, your mother or another person had succeeded in **reaching the goal** of getting rid of you? Can you allow yourself to contemplate this truth? Can you imagine that after the first shock of the threat to life a child's soul can only worry about how it can prevent the adults from achieving their goal? Do you now understand that this must never happen under any circumstances even today? Goosebumps? Can you imagine that a child threatened like this had to constantly slow down or re-direct any action impulses by others? It could never know what would happen next and what dangers lay in the objectives of adults.

Note:
An affected child's soul obtains the lasting impression through its own experience that adults obviously aim to kill small children. In order to survive as a child at that time, no person in your environment could <u>achieve their goal</u> – which was potentially life-threatening for you. For the same reason no adult was allowed then to <u>succeed</u> in what they were doing!

Since you are reading these lines here now you have obviously managed to avert the "worst" at least.

The only question is: at what price?

As a replacement for killing impulses which were derailed or not carried out to conclusion, people often choose physical and mental abuse, often in combination with sexual abuse. Inevitably, children's souls learn very quickly that "distraction" means a chance to survive. The trauma suffered through the threat to life therefore inevitably leads to further emotional splits.

Even if you could not understand these circumstances as a child, each life-threatening experience and intent to kill has marked your soul deeply. Now you are an adult yourself. Your childhood happened a long time ago. You may not have any conscious memories anymore. But your soul definitely has not forgotten about one thing:

Adults must not succeed in achieving their goals, otherwise *you* have to die!

Could it be that you are now an adult yourself who is not successful in the things you do? Do you really believe this is down to you or a "curse"? It is perhaps only because you have learned at an early age what guarantees your survival – and somehow you have always survived until now - haven't you?

Another aspect is the energy of violence, destruction, maltreatment or experiences of previous abuse which is stored in every cell. Even if children are exposed to this just once, their whole being, body system and psyche will be flooded almost completely with impressions of annihilation, destruction and death. The inevitability of events and simultaneous helplessness activates a survival mechanism which leads to the suppression and splitting off of these experiences in the psyche. This is the only way it is possible to survive and carry on living. As adults we might not be able to remember anything. Our life does however still reflect the split-off experience of annihilation, destruction and near death stored in our body system. A part of us is influenced by the perpetrator's energy from our past and still entangled in a cycle of destruction via perpetrator-loyal fragments (another survival structure). This affects our lives like a "sabotage virus". We want nothing to do with the perpetrator's violence but we have to arrange ourselves somehow to survive. In adult relationships this unresolved trauma continues to live on.

For the self-employed, their company might always be teetering between "life and death" or at a constant risk of bankruptcy. As an employee you may increasingly be subject to disregard, harassment and attacks "below the belt". This complex topic alone would probably provide enough material for a whole book.

In my experience, positive thinking and working until you drop does not help in this situation. This topic is a matter for trauma therapists, provided there is an appropriate childhood experience.

Each person is unique and develops their individual survival structures.

If an infant is faced with the task of averting the killing intentions of close caregivers, this is basically an impossible task. That is why I would like to discuss the possible development and significance for the later adult in more detail. Let us return to our initial example.

Your success today apparently threatens another part of your soul which was split off very early and has not realised that another part of it is already an adult. Even today, this soul fragment separated in fear of death is only able to secure its survival by sabotaging the success of closely related adults. The adult who is closest to this fragment today is you of course. That's why you have become the biggest threat to it today. You could also say that you have come too close for comfort to this childhood soul fragment.

This soul part is not able to distinguish between "good" and "bad" – between less and very dangerous adults. The only thing it knows is: the closer an adult gets to it, the more it has to watch out, the more dangerous it can become. The closer an adult gets to it, the more it has control them and impede them. The farther an adult is from it, the safer that part feels.

This is not a joking matter. This is about pure survival!

And if you can push aside your anger about the many years of "sabotage" for a moment, you might notice how perfectly this part of you has been working. You have failed to achieve some goals but you have survived. This part alone has secured your survival! I know this is hard but without proper acknowledgement and appreciation of this exceptional performance you will not be able to move on. It is time to afford this part some loving attention. Remind yourself again and again why this part is suspicious of adults – including yourself. Time has stopped for it. It still feels that it is in mortal danger and adults represent a threat. So be patient and have compassion for yourself. Your greatest success in life will be to reconnect with this part in a healthy way. Through this new "partnership", life energy which has been shackled for a long time will flow freely again and flood all areas of life with joy. Then you will be able to have unlimited success with what you do as an adult without that other soul part inside you feeling threatened by it.

Do not worry. The process of working through the issue is less about the exploration of details of the truth of your childhood but more about the clarification and recognition of a spiritual split. The inner image of your soul is the only interesting truth that should be taken seriously, no matter how much reality and fantasy may have got mixed up together back then in order to ensure your survival.

Before you set out on your journey, you should be aware of the following:

A soul fragment split off from you that may have been separated from you for decades is not the slightest bit interested in share prices, financial matters or business success. Affection, compassion, love, trust and honesty are the levels at which you can meet this part of yourself. That way you gradually recover a very important part of yourself. On the "level of a small child" you can only communicate through authentic feelings and build up a new "climate" of confidence.

If this is your topic, I wholeheartedly wish you the best success.

With this strong partner by your side, the achievement of new targets will be "child's play".

PS:

The part of you that has been taking care of your survival since childhood and since the first life-threatening experience has since then been constantly trying to control and foresee the activities of all adults who come too close and may be dangerous. It has developed several techniques for it. I would like to call one of them "spiritual freezing". What is it? If the "spirit" learns to work faster than its environment is moving, everything practically runs in "slow motion" and there is enough time left to "respond". This way, life constantly moves at a very manageable speed. You could also call it "snail's pace" or "slow motion". I have always felt and described it as going along with the handbrake on. It is a feeling as if it should take ten people to push a balloon.

Since everything happens extremely slowly there are hardly any visible changes in later life. Things that for others might happen within a week will perhaps take even a year for such people.

As an adult you feel completely frustrated in life and do not even partially understand what is going on and how it is happening. Another part of you is highly satisfied with the results. Only you yourself are not.

Does this seem familiar to you?

With your "seventh sense" and your very forward-thinking style as a leader, manager, advisor or coach you are the ideal person to lead others to the success which remains unattainable to you in this form for as long as you do not understand the background connections.

The success of others and the achievement of goals by others are further away from you and thus already less dangerous for the part of you which remains loyal to its "success principles". After all, these principles have already proven themselves very well in securing your survival! Is this clear enough?

For you as an adult this may seem neither sensible nor logical but you cannot approach childlike parts with logic. The only thing that helps is to develop a feeling for the still existing, emotional reality of permanent danger and threat. To this day, this has not gone away for the split, traumatised soul fragment!

If it is only ever enough to survive and there is no lack of personal involvement, an existential trauma is often behind the persistent success blockages. That means at least an event which was a matter of life and death for you or someone close to you. Of course, I do not know what abilities you had to develop as a child in order to survive. I merely wish to give you suggestions which are based on my personal experiences. Perhaps these impulses might help you to discover, understand and appreciate the "secrets to success" as perceived by your childhood soul parts.

I wish from the bottom of my heart that as an adult, you will be able to use these abilities in another form in order to surmount previous limits of life with joy. Maybe the next part will also help you to break out of the previous "prison" and to destroy existing barriers, including mental ones.

Point of Reference:
Everything you have achieved so far is an
important and helpful prerequisite for your
personal success and breakthrough. Do not give
up. Devote yourself to the unknown part inside
you and release it from its task to prevent the
success of the adult closest to it in order
to survive.

Questions that can change your life:

Which "force" could be greater than your creativity, ingenuity and all your years of tireless efforts?

Who or what is "protecting" you from becoming rich and / or famous? Why? Unspecified fear of the public sphere?

What exactly must never become publicly known?

Which taboo of your family system might be touched upon here?

Let the part inside you which knows all this spontaneously complete the following sentences.

Very important! Do not judge the statement! Write down the information immediately which spontaneously comes into your mind first:

- I would rather forego all that money, the fame and personal freedom than / before…

- No matter what I do I will never be able to make up for…

Take these examples as an impulse to spontaneously develop your own sentences.

If other people always harvest your fruits – what offset are we actually talking about here?

On whose behalf did you take the responsibility to compensate for anything?

How many years have you already been fighting for every Cent? 10, 15, 20 years or more?

Whose "guilt" could be so great that a "life sentence" is still too short? What kind of "pledge" or "legacy" are we really talking about here? Are you sure that you have not confused the "construction site" in the symbiosis of childhood? Where might you have been a witness and had to suppress and forget it?

What force works inside you, in your psychical structure which seems to stand "beyond" your life, beyond your goals and desires?

Which type of force or affecting event still takes away the breath of your life?

Which type of force or formative event still makes you freeze in mid-action whenever you do anything, before you even really get going?

The only things that stand above all that leads to life are "death" and the force which, instead of giving and supporting life, ends it and takes it away.

Can you think of specific events in your own biography of which you yourself are a conscious witness and which can justify and explain such success blockages?

If the fight for pure survival simply never seems to stop for you there probably is a part of your personality inside you which is still stuck in its battle for survival.
Allow yourself to ask bold questions.

The human psyche contains fascinating mechanisms which it can use to block out everything in our memories what is connected to traumatic events. As a consequence of these "blind spots" we often face situations, influences and experiences in later life that affect us as if they were controlled by "higher forces". Do not rack your brains if this happens. Seek the contact and the help of those who have appropriate knowledge of trauma.

Deathly Breeze

The fire is barely burning,
a cool breeze comes
and takes your breath
away completely.
Year after year
it becomes more difficult
to rekindle a fire
from the dying embers.

Nobody is surprised;
only I
know
there is something
that created
this coldness long ago.

How much fear does it take
to make everything freeze
that is longing for life so silently?

Hush,
no one must hear us
and know
that we are still here.

Private and State Prison

Since a child is not able to flee for a long time, an environment of violence, abuse and threat is most comparable to the situation of a convict detained in prison. For a child growing up in such a "climate", its home and the closeness to parents and important caregivers is marked by a feeling of imprisonment. Each traumatic event during this time is inseparably connected to the parents or close caregivers. To be connected to the parents means to be imprisoned.

The part of the person that wants to be close to the parents later will often voluntarily go back into "prison" in order to achieve that. Not everyone remains as innocent as the small child was back then. In this context it is worth noting that a prison guard also voluntarily spends most of his life behind bars.

Without help, all you have "lost" through psychological splits in your childhood will be difficult to find again in a state prison. There is however always a part in each personality that wants to understand its life story. This part also senses that, for this purpose, it has to go back to the place where it happened, the period of childhood.

If we want to remember something that we have forgotten as adults, we look for parallels and impressions which can help us to activate the memory. If we have lost something we retrace our steps back to the places where we have been. A part within us may still know that it was a place and time where we were provided with food, sleep, activity and visits. Often the feeling of being "locked up" in a box with bars is also part of the memory. We just no longer know what exactly happened there.

Since these phenomena exist on all social levels there is also the so-called "golden" cage.

And you?
Might you have consciously or unconsciously developed the idea of having been swapped at birth at the hospital? Are you "by chance" spending a lot of time in a hospital now as an adult, professionally, as a visitor or a patient? If not – which idea are you following without being able to say exactly why?

How and where are you searching for your truth, or have you already given up? Do you prefer to follow the truths of others?

Perhaps you have already been searching all your life, all over the world, in many relationships and professions. What for exactly? For the connection to you real parents? For lost, unknown siblings or another child? For ultimate love? You do not know exactly what you are searching for but you are sure that you will recognise it when you find it? All these are possible indicators of TRAUMA.

We often search for our own identity without even knowing it. In this book you have already learnt about some healthy steps in this direction.

Goals, Evolution and Partnership

There is the idea that the goal of evolution is to convert all karmic energies from interpersonal relationships into insight and knowledge and to achieve once again the original complete, balanced, androgynous state – the unity of female and male soul parts and their fusion with other elements into a great whole. Whatever you might think about it, some questions will arise in any case.

What is actually behind karmic energies?

What is behind the principle of Karma?

Who created the principle anyway?

Why is partnership necessary in a karmic sense anyway?

The chain of questions could be continued endlessly. Ultimately, however, the question about the meaning of "where from" and "where to" of the human being remains.

In their search for explanations, human beings do not only tend to put the blame on other people; they also try to find the origin of their Self in faraway places and earlier lives. This often happens because the inconceivability of the truths offered to us by this life blocks the view towards answers which lie much closer. Even I felt the same despite my extensive therapeutic training. Some truths hit us with such tremendous force that we first have to develop a sufficient mental maturity before we are able to grasp them. On your way, trust especially your personal feeling and **in the long term** trust the joy in your life as a measure.

Every doctor who only recommends medication as an answer deserves to be considered with caution **and** healthy mistrust. He probably never learnt any better and hasn't questioned it either.

Making sure you find other answers is solely your responsibility. Information such as you find in this book will hopefully bring a true and "happy" partnership closer for you in a healthy way. Most of all, trust yourself and your feeling. This can also mean to say: I love you and at the same time I feel a sadness inside me that I have not been aware of in this way before.

Whichever ways we chose, whatever we seek, topics such as love, relationship and partnership will always remain a driving force in our luggage, consciously or unconsciously. Many answers to these issues are hidden in the secrets of our childhood and family.

The "karmic part" of a relationship is often influenced by a traumatic childhood in its origin or is connected to it.

We meet a lot of people on our journey and sometimes we have the uncertain feeling that we should retreat. It is helpful to know in these situations that the desire for distance is a part of a healthy survival mechanism. Respect such impulses but also find out about their true origin; otherwise your partner might one day distance themselves from you in order to give you room to think. If this has already happened, you must first of all delete the term "guilt" from your life concept as it connects you unnecessarily to a victim and perpetrator structure which does not offer a way out. Personal freedom and fulfilled partnerships start beyond this structure, by building up a completely new relationship to your personal responsibility for all effects in your life. I truly hope you can find all the courage you need to take on this responsibility.

I hope this guide can provide you with new impulses again and again on your way to leading karmic and other relationships into a new divine freedom.

> ## Note:
> **If secrets from your childhood show up on this journey of discovery, it might be useful to gain a healthy distance to your parents.
> If that is the case, do not hesitate to provide your inner child with the protection which your parents never had the honour to appreciate.**

Where love

comes to its limits

you have to

follow

the flow of time with courage

until the moment

where understanding

gains room

inside us

and

wisdom easily turns to

experience.

02/05/1999

318

The Limits of a Karmic Relationship

Each relationship comes up against the limits of one's own truth from childhood someday.

Naturally it remains a secret until we are ready to lift the veil of all the beautiful stories about a happy childhood.

The limits of your karmic relationship are also significantly determined by secrets which you had to forget at some point in order to survive.

The more perplexed, upset and helpless you feel with it, the stronger your contact with parts of childhood confusion and overburdening probably is. If a partnership situation has caused this and put your "ideal world" into question, the topics love and relationship in your childhood had probably been influenced by confusion and feelings of helplessness. Here, some unimaginable forces are connected in trauma which can develop their own explosive dynamics in suppression and ignorance. These forces often only lose their life-threatening character when the partner who is in more intensive contact with the life-threatening component initiates the separation. These energies of destruction sometimes literally stand in the room. The fear that something bad may happen and the desire to protect the partner leave no choice for the person who feels this threat. In such situations, the separation is neither partner's fault. It is equally awful for both of them even if it helped to prevent something even worse.

The special trust between you and the deep devotion both of you feel towards each other may have led you to touch the "limits" and "guards" of a "taboo", the existence of which neither of you was aware of. That's why you were not in any way prepared for the protective mechanism at this "limit of your relationship". You probably lacked any means or information you would have needed in order to respond to the events that overwhelmed you in any other way. However, by separating and "discharging" this energy, the basic issue is neither recognised nor solved. The survival Selves of both persons are not interested in this particular matter either. Even at the cost of the partnership, they "protect" the access to the trauma with which you came into contact as a couple. Where necessary, a separation is the lesser evil for the survival Self. Therefore, reconciliation and a new start do not last for long in cases of such dynamics; the next separation is inevitable. Some couples keep following the same pattern for years without understanding the deeper connections.

I hope this guide has provided you with plenty of methods to better classify the phenomena of your relationships and to really change your experiences for the better. Every step in this direction is beneficial. Simply keep going. I am not claiming that this is easy. It is possible though. Bring your sad stories to a happy ending. Then the heaven on earth will indeed be free for you and your relationships.

Wonder

I admire your courage
to take life
in your hands again today
with new hope,
although you almost
lost it yesterday.

I am astounded again and again
at the way your love shines
out of your heart
and your words,
although nobody ever taught you
how to do that.

I love you
without a doubt
for the way you keep
your unwavering strength
and belief in yourself.
I know
that this treasure inside you
only needs your love
in order to light up
the narrow path in front of you
against all shadows.

Always remember:
A light is shining towards you,
out of my heart
into the night.
10/12/2009

Checklist for Part 7 – What Exactly Can You Do Right Now?

Step 7

Clearing Up of Your Karmic Relationships

Before we come to the practical part now, there is something else I would like to mention here in order to remove as many boundaries to the exercises as possible.

Especially the "revocation of black magic" naturally causes certain fears and uncertainty. Without additional information such as you can find below, you might miss out on using the exercise to your advantage.

I hope you recognise the significance of this for yourself as a strong opportunity to free your relationships from eternally binding structures.

Divine Freedom – A Key to Unconditional Love and to Revocation of "Black Magic"

The system of black magic works, among others, with the principles of power, manipulation, fear, oppression, illness, enslavement and misfortune.

Anyone who consciously or unconsciously works with energy structures and types of bonds which bind other persons or beings (including animals) to eternal dark fate without freedom has left the protective space of divine freedom and unconditional love. In such cases, a fulfilled, happy love relationship in mutual freedom is no longer possible.

You may mention the world "love" here but not out of the deep feeling of an honest heart. You will know what I mean.

You might even have trained sex-slaves who think they enjoy serving you - love will not warm up your heart no matter how strong the lust is. The way you are arranging your personal life-style may not even include feelings like love as primary aims. Should you however wish to attain the experience of unconditional love, your "revocation of black magic" will be an important first step in that direction. Why is this necessary? That's simple. You cannot create any room for divine freedom and unconditional love if you're obliged to work within structures of manipulation and dependency. Neither can you enter a white room with "black feet" without being noticed.

Do you always find yourself in unfree love relationships and would like to change that? You do not remember when and how you got entangled in experiments and experiences with the dark side of the force? - You are not alone there and in order to understand this it is helpful to address the model of previous lives.

The human soul loves to make new experiences, to experiment with its own and other forces in the universe. Often neither short nor long-term consequences can be foreseen.

Science still teaches and learns this way even today and is willing to accept that parts of nature, humans or animals are badly damaged or die due to such experiments and learning phases. The higher the ethics of a society, the greater the benefit of such experiences can be in the long-term.

If you always end up with the same unsatisfying results today despite numerous experiments in the area of relationships, you have not concluded the process of

- **analysis** (what have I done, how and why?),

- **change** (what could I do differently in order to change the result?),

- **development** (what have I learnt so far?),

- **creativity** (what haven't I thought of until now?), and

- **realisation** (essence, core message – what do all results have in common and why?)

in such a way that a satisfying result could be achieved. In quantum physics it has been scientifically proven that the mental attitude of the person who carries out certain experiments significantly influences the possible results. So what is this to do with a happy love relationship and all that "black magic stuff"? It's quite simple. If, to stay with the grounded, scientific approach, you want to create conditions which contain the component "love" as a result of your relationship experiments, it is helpful for you as the person who carries out the experiment not to exclude the desired result by way of your mental attitude, consciously or unconsciously.

Since "love" is a very diffuse factor, the factors affecting it might also be of a rather "diffuse" nature. I would therefore like to invite you to review your basic mental attitude, your ethics and your karmic history in relation to the aspects of your desired outcomes. Just as if this was a scientific project. It may well be that there are significant parts which you have never questioned or taken into account before. This is also about resolving anything we have internalised as unconscious fears.

I do not know your personal circumstances of course. During my research I have however noticed certain connections and factors which have a significant influence on the areas of partnership, relationship and love. In the course of my own "analysis-change-development-creativity-realisation-processes" I have also developed exercises which bring one's own basic mental attitude back to a state of independence and freedom which I also call "divine freedom".

At this point I would like to clarify the terms I used here:

The "divine freedom" I am talking about here existed long before all kinds of belief systems derived their business models from it. Divine freedom is a universal, indestructible right which does not need to be organised.

The "divine freedom" I am talking about here is not part of any of organisations known to me. An autonomous divine freedom is not something that agrees with the worldwide belief systems and their business executives.

The term "ritual" can mean a lot of different things. I use this term within the exercises as a clear indicator of a conscious, self-responsible, mental attitude and work of consciousness in terms of self-transformation and freedom. My aim here is to support your inner orientation and a healthy seriousness which has nothing to do with religion or esotericism.

Your inner attitude when participating in traditional rituals in our society such as Fasching or New Year's Eve will also most certainly be different to your attitude to your own wedding preparations.

For your orientation, that last example seems to me quite appropriate in terms of the exercises. The energy of a conscious new decision you have made yourself also activates inner unconscious forces which facilitate a good solution. Feel free, if necessary, to use your own terms which help you to make the best use of the exercises for yourself.

All karmic relationships described in this guide have at some point in their history lost this divine freedom. According to my experience, this divine freedom can only be regained with divine help and a complete "revocation of black magic". You also need the light and help of divine mercy in order to be able to give back their freedom to all victims of your experiments with the dark side of the force, as you will hardly be able to re-member all details. Even if you still remember one or another curse you have uttered or you remember a thought with a curse spoken out loud – the dissolution of these energy structures was probably not included in the "user guide".

But as long as there are still "victims" who are caught in eternally binding energy structures which you have created at some point, your own life will be a mirror of this lack of freedom. The sooner you remember and consider the full ramifications of these connections, the faster you will feel the unconditional love of divine freedom in your heart.

The more people follow this way, the faster they will all live together in a society where happy relationships in unconditional love and divine freedom have their firm place. And there is only one thing to do to achieve it: Roll your sleeves up! Are you up for it?

You might still be not aware of this but your personal "space" is influenced by your entire karmic story – whether you remember it or not. Even experiments and previous contracts with the dark side of the force by members of your family system leave their traces behind and radiate into your environment. Your new mental attitude in this life – no matter how full of light it may be – is definitely not enough here in order to dis-solve these previous bonds and entanglements created by the family system. This requires you to take a new, clear, unique and very conscious decision which sees things for what they really are! Without your revocation of black magic the divine level is not allowed to dissolve the binding structures which had been created by you. Without your explicit request for help directed at the divine mercy, the light of divine mercy will not be active for you as only you can decide whether you really want it. This is about your own free, divine will. Do you want to carry on as before or do you want to try another "experiment"? This is entirely your decision!

Although I am trying to bring this topic closer to you in a light-hearted way, this is a very serious matter of vast significance. This will be a struggle for you despite all the divine help, half-hearted decisions and empty phrases will therefore not suffice here! At this turning point there is only "Either-Or". There is however a kind of "grey zone" in between, for people who want to move from one "side" to the other right now. Perhaps you have the feeling that you have been in such a zone for a while already, despite the fact that you have always had a divine orientation in this life. That's because although you have made your internal decision to change course, you have not yet carried out the "revocation of black magic" with a strength which has an external effect.

I am aware that the term "black magic" may be rather alarming for you. This fact alone demonstrates the influence of this term which has been used for centuries. For me, there are only energy structures which have been created with different intentions. In this guide we use a term which has been developed throughout centuries to dissolve a structure which works with manipulation, damage spells and dependencies of all kinds.

8 Helpful Steps for Your Reference:

1. Your inner transformation, new orientation and decision.

2. Saying aloud your "revocation of black magic" in the face of the divine source. The conscious ending of a magical and manipulative life-style. Stepping out of a world influenced by magical thinking.

3. Your new commitment to the "divine source" and "divine freedom" in unconditional love.

4. Your dissolution of all previous, eternally binding energy structures with divine help.

5. Your recognition and willingness to take full responsibility for the damage you have caused until now.

6. Your honest willingness to say "sorry" to the "victims" of your previous life-style. This is all about an inner attitude and an inner process which neither demands nor has as a goal an external encounter or absolution.

7. The willingness to ensure adequate compensation for any damage caused. The divine level will lead you wisely during this process – let go of the idea that this will or must happen 1 : 1 (you will find a link to a tip on reconciliation at the end of this book).

8. Forgive yourself for everything that has been blessed and led to a new order in the light of the divine mercy.

These are steps recommended by me which have proven themselves useful in practice.

Repeat each step in your own way until it feels concluded.

The exercises and texts in the practical part below are meant as tools for orientation. If you have difficulties with the term "black magic", find something else that is more appropriate for you. It is about dissolving eternally binding energy structures which are intended to harm others and to manipulate them. The abovementioned term has evolved in mass consciousness over centuries. You can use this advantage in the exercise for clear and unambiguous demarcation. That way you also include the influences and experiences of past lives in a very effective way, in which you may have lived and acted using this terminology.

My intention here is not to enter into discussions about black, white or "rose-tinted" magic. I would like to support you in improving the quality of the energy structures in which you are living. An important step into personal freedom and autonomy is the separation from manipulative energy structures which other people may also have tied you to – no matter when or how.

My goal here isn't to discuss earlier or future lives either. There is no scientific proof of this as yet. However, it seems to me to be helpful – for similar reasons as with "black magic" – to include this possibility into the personal work-up. If we include this idea, you can also use the possibilities of transformation which are connected to it. I deliberately follow the pragmatic approach here and recommend that you "clean up" "past lives" as well, just in case. It won't do any harm in any case. Decide for yourself.

You are welcome to develop your own method from the transformation texts and let the results prove the effectiveness. Please remain very, very critical while doing so!!! The dark side is very devious and master of illusionary worlds and feelings. Faced with the divine source it must however show its colours very quickly. Whatever may be. I wish you the courage to change and the strength to follow your path to the end, into the light of divine freedom. From this point onwards it will be easier for you to clean up the "broken pieces" behind you. With this new "personal space" you will attract a partner who took similar steps in order to be able to feel their heart in unconditional love. This love will doubtlessly be blessed in the light of the divine source.

Do you feel that you are worth it to embrace this love? Then let's go!

Do not go to sleep today before you have found a vision which is worth getting up for tomorrow.

10/09/1999

First Aid for Separations in Karmic and Other Relationships

Part I: 23 Rules, Information and Guidance for Abandoned People

1. **Do not take it personally** – this is not about degrading your person, on the contrary.

2. **Rest assured that it prevented something even worse.**

3. **Realise** that you are worth being protected in this way and thank the (divine) source which may be unknown to you for its help. Forget about the external circumstances. They only create the opportunity to rescue the other from the karmic relationship before the "time bomb" explodes. The karmic pattern that both of you still carry with you is an "explosive" you now have to defuse calmly. This separation stopped the countdown.

4. **If Karma is placed into the stream of time** and can be experienced by you as fate, you are prompted directly and personally to bring this event into a new divine order. The quickest way to achieve this is not to apportion blame. Activate your inquiring mind with the aim to detect and dissolve initial causes. Neutralise your part in the issue of "unhappy love". Here, I can only recommend that you include experienced guides, trauma constellations and perhaps also regression in order to gain clarity, distance and an overview.

5. **Any form of** "**love ritual**" performed in order to revoke the separation and to get the partner back is black magic and any "success" will, as a rule, be short-lived. Only the quality of manipulation, misuse and unhappiness in your relationship will become stronger this way and will have the effect of an additionally burdening and eternally binding force. You thus only aggravate the situation further and attract new misfortune! Keep well away from this, even if it is difficult for you. If you have already performed such a ritual ask or had it performed on your behalf, ask the divine force to revoke it / make it invalid. Use "**revocation of black magic**" as a guide for this purpose.

6. **For any bad thoughts that are or have developed** as well as curses against your partner, **send** at least two good ones, and ask the divine order for energetic neutralisation. This point is very important because you will otherwise start a new karmic bond which could possibly be worse than the one which already exists.

7. **The person who left you** has, as a rule, been isolated from you in another karmic maelstrom and they already have more than enough to do with themselves. I know it is not easy for you to understand but the drama of another person can only be completely revealed to them by the divine source in your absence.

8. **Along with the separation itself this is** the first most important part of a test for you as an abandoned person. Now the divine source can reveal to

you the whole dimension of your karmic entanglement.

9. **If you look at your personal situation and story more closely** you will discover important puzzle pieces in your life relationships which point to forces which have already been accompanying you for some time and are much bigger than you or the other person. Perhaps you remember one thing or another or have experienced something similar before.

It might for example be:
- impulsive energies of separation like a thunderstorm and then everything calms down again

- nightmares which you have experienced while you were together with your partner

- friendships which have ended abruptly, inexplicably and suddenly by accidental death, flight from life, "lost on a journey" or other circumstances

- earlier loss of a beloved person whom you are still mourning

Search for ways and possibilities to gain deeper understanding of what the real cause of all these entanglements is. Use the new methods of trauma therapy as well. Make sure that you do not take these issues with you again in further lives. You will succeed.

10. **Take good care of yourself and the other person.** Face the challenge in this life with the certainty that there is a beneficial divine order which honours all beings in unconditional love. If you do not feel this unconditional love or the new divine freedom yet, it means that you have not yet successfully completed some essential points of this test. Always know that no matter what happens – a part of you knows the truth and the way to a new freedom. The "guilt of the other" is often based on his "innocence" with which he has prayed for divine help for both of you. The higher council also calls it "**the application**". It is the basis for a chain of events as it is described here. If you trust the other person to have lodged such an "application", please go on to reading item 11.

11. **Wish the other luck on their journey**; if the journey of discovery should fail we cannot hand over the karmic key in this life which opens the gate to the dissolution of your karmic pattern.

12. **Do everything that's necessary** in order to end the drama of your karmic relationship. Lodge your own "application" in the face of the divine in the sense of: "**Please release me from this**". The "divine" will honour every serious application! "Fasten your seatbelt and trust the things to come".

13. **Let yourself be surprised.** Open yourself to a new divine order which can also show itself beyond your current desires and longings (which are still influenced by the drama).

14. **Make a conscious decision** to live once again and put away all conscious or unconscious thoughts and energies to end your life early. Use the **"revocation of all bonds to death, dying and the dark sides of life"** as a help for this – see also the following exercises.

15. **Make a conscious** new decision for the principal direction and style of your life. Use the **"revocation of black magic"** as a help for this.

16. **Convert the** dark shadows of your history in a divine way, step by step. As a help, you can repeatedly use the **"ritual of mental purification of heart and body"** as well as the **"rituals of forgiveness"**.

17. **The forces which have led to your unhappy experience today** are very complex and diverse. They will remain active until you feel a deep unconditional love in your heart which includes the other person. Only when you do not need the other person anymore in order to feel good or bad, you have dissolved the structures of dependency and energy which are the cause of each unfree unhappy karmic love relationship.

18. **Embark on your journey, go off and regain the quality of your divine origin.** Then I promise you that you will discover the separation as a big gift and appreciate it. Each separation is about yourself in the first place and about the answer you will give your life this time! Others often only help to increase the desire for you to make fundamental changes at

last. Find the answers which deeply touch on the essence of your being and explain the meaning of other people within it. Through recognition, this path always leads to a new form of personal freedom and love.

19. **For the sake of completeness:** After a separation, mental sexual contacts and fantasies with the former partner have the character of rape and strictly speaking mean sexual abuse. This is not about burgeoning memories of beautiful encounters in a time of a mutual love relationship but the conscious reaching for another body in order to satisfy one's own lust without having the other person's consent for it - who you are now separated from. Be aware that you will create new bonds by doing this and delay the process of clearing up the separation. The "sexual dependence" on each other, if it exists, must also be dissolved completely as it also carries in itself the seed of the unfree, unhappy love.

20. **If despair** and longing are overwhelming you, always remember one thing: Without diminishing all the positives, you yourself were not truly happy deep inside. If you are honest with yourself and the other, you will know that the other has not left your joint illusion of a perfect world because of you. Perhaps you allow yourself to assume that your partner set out to search for a lost ability to feel happiness and love that you have also lost one day. A long time before this relationship had started.

21. **All earlier attempts to separate** reflect the lack of freedom to be able to live together in unconditional

love and happiness. Now the separation finally gives you the chance to break through the karmic circle. Both of you bear the responsibility for the dissolution of your karmic entanglement.

22. **It is not your fault**!
Stop reproaching yourself or racking your brains asking what you have done wrong.
It is most certainly nothing to do with your age or your appearance or the sex with you. On the contrary! It is because you are appreciated and you are special that someone is ready to shoulder the biggest and most difficult trials of their life now.

Do you really believe that the separation is easy for the other person? That they can finally fully enjoy their life now, perhaps in a new partnership? If that were the case, this is no karmic relationship and unhappy love in the sense of this guide. Before you draw premature conclusions, I would like you to carefully think about this question: Is your former partner really as superficial as the answer with which you made do until now?

23. **If your former partner** has already met you with aspects of humiliation, contempt, violence, abuse and manipulation at another time, the separation will reveal your own weariness of the false game. In such a case you were used from the beginning. You should be glad that this is over now. Do not waste your time any longer with the other person. Concentrate on clearing up and dissolving the original entanglement with the above aspects.

Take responsibility for apparently unclarified events you encountered as a "mirror" in the context of the partnership. Where do betrayal, violence, humiliation, contempt, abuse or manipulation have their origins? This is the essential question in terms of this separation.

Any tendency to chase after the other person is your refusal to face your own personal shadows from earlier times right now. You are free to decide the direction of your life!

If you are aiming for some form of unconditional love, it is helpful to dissolve the "victim-perpetrator cycle" at its own karmic root. A free happy love relationship is only possible if you dissolve all dependencies between perpetrator and victim roles. You can only dissolve the entanglement with a "perpetrator" in the long-term if you are ready for unconditional love of yourself. For better understanding please read the section on "Karmic Relationship between Victim and Perpetrator" further on.

Part II: 17 Rules and Guidelines for Those Who Have Ended a Relationship

1. **Continue to trust your impulse.**
   It was right. But do not stay there as time alone never can heal these wounds.

2. **I know that the consequences of your separation** are one of the biggest challenges in your life to date. For a very long time, perhaps for many years, you will be able to rely solely on the part of mental clarity which has led you to the path of change to achieve perfect healing. A time in which you cannot rely on many of your feelings anymore because otherwise you would go back immediately.

3. **Most likely you can compare** this to a captain caught in his worst storm surge who steers his ship back on course again and again despite that uneasy feeling and under extreme tension in order to save what is sacred to him. Some forces hit us with such force that our life becomes a very narrow ridge where the only hope is just to keep running forwards.

4. **Conflicting feelings**, confusion, self-accusations, doubts, incomprehension and many questions without names will be your closest companions for a long time now. Without the ability to be uncomfortable in yourself up to the pain threshold you will easily get lost on this path.

5. **The temptation to give up** and to turn back to the dependency and limitation of a familiar, comfortable

340

pretence of happiness will accompany you like an addict in withdrawal. Only you can muster the will and the discipline to be strong for this one day today and to carry on. Prepare a spiritual road of hope ahead of yourself, every single day, which you can walk along. The power that wants to pull you back is the power of a fate which was born in ignorance and unhappiness. The stronger the pull of this power, the greater your addiction-like dependencies still are. It is precisely these karmic structures that need to be dissolved.

6. **Look for ways and possibilities** to understand more deeply what contains the real cause of all these entanglements. Use the new methods of trauma constellation as well. Make sure that you do not take this issue with you again into a future life. Right now you are closer than ever before to a comprehensive transformation. You will do it.

7. **Honour the separation**, the love, the partner by carefully continuing on your way and carrying your responsibility in dignity. I know this is easier said than done. Pluck up all your courage in the certainty that a protective power leads and accompanies you if you are looking for divisive factors with a sincere heart, factors which - like explosives - still form a minefield in your life.

8. **Please also read Part I, "Rules, Information and Guidance for Abandoned People"** and look at the contents as befits your situation. It is important to accept the part inside you that feels abandoned because there is certainly an as yet unhealed

experience as an abandoned person from earlier times, a repeat of which you perhaps just managed to avoid.

9. **It is normal** for you to feel alone on your lonely journey, even in a new relationship. Please respect the opportunities to heal your history that this partnership contains. Always and very consciously show your sincere appreciation to the new person by your side. It is normal that this often does not succeed in the emotional depth and spontaneity which you also know from your personal experience.

10. **Make particular use of the exercises at the end.**

11. **When the waves become calmer** and you have survived the worst of the storm, you will need long breaks and rest periods. When the ground beneath your feet becomes firmer again and your breath flows easier, it is time to give a new space to your feelings. Perhaps you might be "lucky" then and find someone by your side who helps you to rediscover life like a new language. In any case, give yourself time to enjoy life again and to trust your feelings again, bit by bit.

12. **As a happy ending** at the end of the path you will find a free relationship that allows you to experience new levels of partnership in unconditional love. Your courage to embark on this journey was just the first step towards this. Be confident that your healing process also nourishes the soul of the person whom you have left at that time. You can leave

everything else safely in the hands of the divine source, without expectation.

13. **Life can only be lived forwards** and understood backwards. You cannot change anything about the way things were. Only now in the present, you can check all your knowledge and insights and give a worthy place in your heart to the events of the past. Even many years later you may still feel a deep gratitude for all the beautiful things that you have experienced in your past relationship. Thank your partner whenever such feelings arise, and let this message ascend into the unknown tied to a spiritual balloon, if you wish. Avoid establishing new direct spiritual contacts at all cost, as this is not appropriate for you anymore. It also injures the dignity of the other person. Communicate exclusively via the divine level and the love in your heart, otherwise there is a risk that you will still continue to maintain old dependencies under the guise of gratitude! In personal contacts through children you have between you or other circumstances you have to stay in harmony with your true divine heart and keep your dignity. Please read the final point in Part I "For the Sake of Completeness" in addition to this.

14. **It is possible that** the love **in your new relationship** is free and beyond doubt now, but that all other qualities and joys of life which have been free in your earlier relationship are seemingly not available to you anymore. You feel your honest, deep love for the new partner but nevertheless you feel totally unhappy, confused and as if at a dead-end of contradictions. At times you might even feel com-

pletely cut off from life and your feelings. Here it is especially important to remind yourself again and again that your separation is the beginning of an important clarification phase to a karmic relationship and not the end of it. The good news is that if you know these feelings you are already holding an important key to freedom in your hands. You have come into contact with the feeling of an ancient split that took place between the love in your heart and your life long before terms such as relationship, partnership or love relationship had a meaning in your consciousness. You live in energies of TRAUMA.

Are you persevering in your deep love without really feeling able to change anything about your life situation? Do you have any idea of what is becoming apparent here? You are probably still living in a survival mechanism from your childhood which was marked by traumatic experiences. Your inability to make a change today reflects in its origin the helplessness of a child who could not change anything and had to endure everything in love in order to survive. Any events that destroy the child's natural trust in caregivers and life can only be survived by a child at the expense of a psychological split.

Why does all this show itself only now? What exactly does it take to be able to carry and transform large shadows? Correct! L o v e - ideally in XXL-format. I could also say: A love is always as big as the shadows that it can carry and transform.

The innocent child's love of that time is now also a heathy part of your new relationship. With the power and capacity you have as an adult now it is up to you to understand the old split between love and life and to dissolve traumatically fixed life patterns. Use the explanations on TRAUMA in Part 5 for it. Talk often and openly about these issues in your relationship. Read some of the recommended books together to expand your horizons and to gain an even bigger understanding for each other. But do not expect an instant solution here.

15. **A core topic in your new partner's life** will probably also appear in your own life story as a traumatic experience. You should at least check this indicator.

Life with trauma is like a fight against dark forces which do not give away an inch of ground or any secret. Trauma constellations in seminars and one-to-one sessions can unlock the "secrets" of your life step by step and convert them into a good power.

16. **If despair** and longing overwhelm you, always remember one thing: You were not happy and therefore your former partner also could not really be happy. You have left the illusion of a perfect world in order to find out the truth about your own lost ability to feel happiness and love. This prompts feelings of mental suffering from the start, the causes of which you will not find in the love relationship you have ended. No matter how strongly you or your former partner may wish for this.

17. If despair and longing overwhelm you, always remember one thing: You have not been happy with all your heart ...

Part III: Background to the Exercises

As a consequence of trauma many people get lost on their "spiritual" search and are in danger of losing their self-perception more and more. Since trauma can only be survived by cutting off, splitting off and suppressing a real, lived experience, any truths which touch on our own or inherited traumas are as a rule ignored during the search for partners and answers to life questions. Our own reality is determined by what may or should be true.

When our own life becomes a taboo zone, we create our own fantasy worlds as a protection zone for ourselves in order to survive. The search and creation of a better world quickly leads to new life concepts and alternative healing methods. Here, everything becomes interesting that explains the world, the creation and our role in all that in a way that does not touch on our trauma. More often than not, "spiritual teachers", "gurus", "channel mediums" and others unconsciously respect this taboo because they are affected themselves. By way of a "rescue", some offer "enlightenment" as the ultimate solution in these spiritual, occult or esoteric circles. This giant leap can be accomplished by only a few people. All the others often spend decades surrounded by the mist of incense sticks of their idols without coming an inch closer to the truth about their own story.

I have personally experienced how such a "sacred" idol died of cancer and took with him all illusions which had been built up until then. Those who look closer might get the idea that "enlightenment" is only the last

347

vanishing point which consciousness can create whilst excluding its own Self.

But how can you get out of your own illusion, confusion and fantasy world in a healthy way? How do we get to really wholesome answers and truths? Undeniably with reasonable speed and sufficient patience. Each diver starts to come up after a long excursion before the oxygen reserves are exhausted. Those who have been in the underwater world for a long time have to patiently pass through the different stages of pressure adaptation. "Shooting up" straight to the surface would be extremely harmful to their health and could even be life-threatening.

This guide is intended as an opportunity to go through various steps to clear up relationships. Spiritual or occult relationships with others and oneself take up a lot of room in some people's lives. With a few specific exercises I would like to offer help to help yourselves here. The form and content of the texts deliberately include the level of unhealthy, entangled relationships and open the way to consciously move a step away from them. In my experience, using specific terms helps to distance oneself from "magical thinking" and related fears. If you are open to therapeutic help, I recommend that in cases of spiritual entanglement you also clear up the background as a personal intention with trauma constellations. That way you will quickly get a clear view of the function and importance of your personal spirituality.

Since I have worked as a spiritual life coach for many years, I know that many people have been traumatised or have traumatised themselves during their search, by coming into contact with spiritual topics, occult groups or sects. In such cases, the exercises might possibly appear threatening to you or awaken bad feelings in you even whilst just reading this book. Pay attention to your feelings and please skip this section if necessary. It will only be a first step for you anyway.

The exercises offered here are meant as an immediate aid with regards to topics which even for many therapists cause uncertainty and anxiety. I would like to provide support to all people in this way who do not yet feel able to put their trust in therapeutic help. Even though I no longer work with these exercises in my practice today, I know that they are perfectly suitable as a form of self-help for many people with a "spiritual history" in order to gain new mental clarity.

As trauma therapist, I would like to pick up people who are looking for my help and assistance at the point they are at right now. My decades of experience in the spiritual sector also have a therapeutic background. I regard this wealth of experience as part of my extensive training in the field of life coaching. As a reader you can find out for yourself whether the following exercises can give you personal incentives, help or orientation.

If you feel that your therapist is a person who is still traumatised by their own history regarding "esotericism", I highly recommend that you find a different person who may deal with this topic without bias. Such an unclarified, burdensome history reveals itself in negative, aggressive attitudes and derogatory remarks regarding "spiritual" experiences you speak about.

From people for whom your spiritual history might represent a "red flag" you can only expect assistance in areas that are not affected by their own unresolved trauma. Trauma therapists are no exception here. This also applies analogously to all other topics which the persons who you seek help from have not cleared up for themselves!

In a good therapeutic consultation you will always get a new reference and alternative views to your personal life story, even and especially when it contains spiritual experiences.

Would you claim that the lava fields on Lanzarote have simply grown out of the ground? Sometimes we are so fascinated by things that we completely lose sight of how they have been created. In order to get closer to the origin of life phenomena and relationship issues it can be very helpful to create an order within "spiritual" life structures and to assume a new point of view. With the following exercises, I would like to invite you to personally make a few new, autonomous decisions. If you do not know what we are talking about here you have developed different survival structures. Simply skip this section. Spirituality is just one of many survival mechanisms and a likely result of trauma.

Part IV: 6 Important Notes on Using the Exercises

1. **Make sure** that you are not disturbed or interrupted whilst doing the exercises. Turn off the phone, mobile, oven etc.

2. **Prepare the room or area** in your own way so that you can provide a "divine" protected environment.

3. **The aim is not** to just get through the exercises but to create a meaningful connection with the particular subject. If you find that you do not feel anything and you are not touched by the issue then perhaps this is not the right time for you to work with it or you have already fully dissolved and integrated the issue in a different way.

4. **The mirror of your life will definitely show you** the truth. In other words: If for example you repeatedly have suicidal thoughts or you feel impulses to self-destruction, your own or foreign "programmes" for the premature end of your life must still exist.

5. **Do not underestimate the effect of these rituals**. Take care when working with the exercises and take note of your inner feelings on when and which exercise you are working with. Leave some room in between for integration. The revocation exercises in particular as a rule caused a strong energy boost for me in practice, which can lead to slight dizziness. This is perfectly normal and should not worry you. If necessary, breathe in and out deeply and

regularly until your energy system calms down. Focus on your feet whilst doing this.

6. **Simply just reading the exercises will not change anything.** Without your active, conscious participation the exercises are like a "recipe". You can make something from it or not. Reading gives you information only. By saying the texts out loud you go into conscious action and activate the keys stored therein.

If you cannot use spoken language, use sign language or paint a picture which lets you transfer the words and the purpose of the exercises into the outer world in your way. Get creative.

Take advantage of those ways to express yourself that are available in your personal life situation. Play an instrument, compose a song, create a sculpture, a building or a theatre play which expresses all your feelings in an individual way. You are unique. The way you do the exercises can be unique too.

You will feel when your "message" has arrived.

If you don't feel confident doing the exercises on your own, ask a suitable, trustworthy person to accompany you.

At this point I would like stress once again that the following exercises do not replace therapeutic counselling. Since I started working with the constellation of the intention according to Prof Dr Franz Ruppert in my practice in 2009 I no longer had any need to use the exercises.

For me, serious counselling includes open, honest communication regarding my therapeutic development. It was a long way from the esoteric / spiritual life coach to becoming a trauma therapist. I would now like to make a few of the steps that have supported me many years ago in finding my way into the next level of my own clarity available to you as evidence and testimony. Perhaps you are now at a similar point as I was then and have been looking for a solution to clear up your "spiritual" relationships for some time.

Those who deny
their past
have not understood it.

05/04/1997

I now trustingly put these exercises in your hands for your own use.

However, the use of the exercises is entirely your own responsibility. At the end of exercise 7 you can also print the exercises via the reader's service.

7 Exercises to Clear up Your Relationships

1) Revocation of All Bonds to Death, Dying and the Dark Sides of Life

Please call and connect with your guardian angel in your own way, as well as your divine leaders and helpers and the divine Self.

If you can, turn inwardly to the Divine Father and the Divine Mother and ask for their help and assistance.

Then speak aloud out of your heart:
In the face of the divine, in the face of the Divine Father and the Divine Mother, I revoke here and now all bonds to death, to premature death and to the dark sides of life that have ever been spoken or left unspoken.

I now choose life once again!

I now choose life once again!

I now choose life once again!

354

... feel it, breath in and out consciously, feel the feet on the ground – observe possible energy and body reactions and let them happen.

I thank the dark companions who have shared my life with me up to now and say goodbye to them in love and freedom.

I thank you all for your closeness, your sympathy and the shared time of sadness and death.

I now turn to life again

and in deep appreciation wish you luck and well-being on your onward journey. May you also be blessed, protected and accompanied by the Divine.

I now turn to life again and cannot give you shelter in it anymore. Please, leave my spaces and my life now and take all your things and sad stories away with you. Until today you were always welcome in my life but now new times are starting for me. Please respect that.

I now choose life once again,

I choose love and joy. I promise to honour the divine gift of life no matter what trials or challenges it may include for me.

Here and now I make a new covenant with life

and promise to do anything that is necessary in order to enjoy it in ease and joy. I ask for the gift of divine mercy to accept me again in life.

… observe your feelings until all possible reactions have normalised again.

Thank you for the gift of my life.

Helplessness, bewilderment, curiosity and desperation often lead towards magical thinking and acting. The following two exercises can help you to consciously break free from the entanglements created this way. The key to the dissolution is above all a conscious new decision and spiritual reorientation.

2) Revocation of Black Magic

This revocation is an option offered by me. It serves as an incentive to start dealing with this particular issue yourself and should be understood as a first step. You hereby make a new decision for a basic life orientation and design. The processing of your karmic and magical history is a whole chapter in itself. This can help to shape the first page of it. I recommend you carry it out in a protected environment.

<u>Recite the text loudly and clearly:</u>

In the face of the divine source – the Divine Father, the Divine Mother and the dark side of the Force – I hereby revoke all my vows, bonds and promises to black magic.

By virtue of my own free will which has never been revoked by God, I now revoke all my vows, bonds, agreements and contracts with the dark side of the force and black magic. With all my heart I ask my creators, the Divine Father and the Divine Mother, to forgive my betrayal of the light and ask to undo all my vows and bonds to black magic – across time and space – across all incarnations – at all levels and in all dimensions.

I beg forgiveness for all the damage caused by my betrayal of the light. I hereby release all souls that I have – in whatever way – ever tied to black magic and beg their forgiveness for all the pain and sorrow that they have experienced because of me. I now accept my part of the responsibility for it and hereby commit myself to putting my life in the service of the divine source of light and unconditional love.

I ask for permission to enter into the strength of my own soul again and I connect myself again completely to 100 percent to the soul that I AM.

I AM a child of the light and serve light and love.

Only unconditional love is free love. Only free love is divine.

Only divine love is pure. May all beings be blessed.

Note:

Without the personal willingness to be touched and affected inwardly it is not possible to obtain the grace and blessing of forgiveness from the divine level.

If you cannot feel the pain and sorrow that others may have experienced because of you, use the feeling of your own pain and sorrow to recognise that others had to experience similar things because of you.

Your personal concern and recognition are the true bridge to salvation.

Similarly, it is advisable to forgive yourself in order to break through the cycle and the pattern of self-punishment. If the divine level has forgiven us, we should not hold on to it any longer either, because that would mean that we presume to stand above the divine.

With the inner attitude of mindfulness, humility and courage for deepest honesty with ourselves, we also get out of the darkest parts of our history into the divine light. The mirror of our present is our greatest teacher here. Now you also know why...

Repeat the ritual, if necessary, until you have the feeling that it has been completed.

You may also want to print this specific text and work with it. At the end of exercise 7 there is a reader's service for this. Then, burn this sheet at an appropriate public fire outside your home!

You can also include specific persons and expand the revocation that way. Now is a good time to pick up your list from Part 2 if you have created one. The following format in exercise 3) is designed and suitable for including people and particular events which you described in step 2 (Checklist for Part 2) for this purpose. Maybe this format is just right for you.

Simply use the following exercise as motivation and, if you want to, develop your own format from it which is suitable for you. If your words, your feelings and your sincere intentions find an authentic form that feels right to you, you will definitely be successful.

If required, change your words, your inner attitude and feelings until you feel a positive "feedback" to your words spoken in "mindfulness and humility".

Perhaps it might also helpful to choose a different setting for this.

3) Dissolution of Eternal Bonds between People

I call on the Divine Father, the Divine Mother and the Divine Source.

I ask the light of divine grace for dissolution of all eternal bonds that still exist between me and (first name / last name / inner image).

Possible extension:

I would also like to include the following persons:

.... (first name / last name / inner image)

.... (first name / last name / inner image)

I hereby revoke all my vows, bonds and promises in the face of the divine source with which I have – whenever – bound m y s e l f to you.

I hereby revoke all my vows, bonds and promises in the face of the divine source with which I have – whenever – bound y o u to myself.

I hereby ask the light of divine grace for us to dissolve in love any eternal forms of black magic bonds which remain between us, now and forever.

I hereby revoke in the face of the divine source – the divine father, the divine mother and the dark side of the force – all my vows, bonds and promises to black magic.

By virtue of my own free will which has never been revoked by God, I now revoke all my vows, bonds, agreements and contracts with the dark side of the force and black magic. With all my heart I ask my creators, the Divine Father and the Divine Mother, to forgive my betrayal of the light and ask to undo all my vows and bonds to black magic – across time and space – across all incarnations – at all levels and in all dimensions.

I beg forgiveness for all the damage caused by my betrayal of the light. I hereby release all souls that I have – in whatever way – ever tied to black magic and beg their forgiveness for all the pain and sorrow that they have experienced because of me.

I now accept my part of the responsibility for it and hereby commit myself to putting my life in the service of the divine source of light and unconditional love.

I ask for permission to enter into the strength of my own soul again and I connect myself again completely to 100 percent to the soul that I AM.

I give thanks, also on behalf of the other persons, for any form of divine assistance.

4) The Release of Your Shadows in a Divine Way

A Ritual for Mental Purification of Heart and Body:

Sit down with your eyes closed in a quiet and safe place where you feel comfortable and relaxed.

Now imagine how you would approach your guardian angel or a trusted divine representative.

Hold your mental hands in front of your heart like a bowl now and let all the dark shadows of your heart flow into your divine hands.

Then give all the dark shadows of your previous life to the Divine Being in front of you and ask it to convert them into love, faith and hope in a divine way.

Repeat the process as many times as necessary until you feel the shining being of your heart again.

Then keep your mental hands at the level of your chest in front of your body like a bowl and let all the dark shadows and energy structures of your body flow together. Imagine how all these energies condense into a kind of energy ball inside you.

Now reach into your body with your mental hands and lift this dark energy ball out of your body.

Lay this part of your past history into the hands of the divine being in front of you as well and ask it to dispose of and convert this energy so that it cannot cause further harm.

Express your gratitude in your own way for this particular form of divine assistance.

04/03/2007

A Characteristic of Karmic Relationships is the "Inevitable".

Surely you also know situations and sequences of events which end in a complete mess, with you right in the middle of it.

I am not talking about the situations in which you might have impulsively thrown a plate against the wall. What I want to discuss here are moments in our lives that virtually pass us by, similar to a film in which we have a role that we are not completely aware of.

I am referring to events that remain in our memory for years and which again and again lead us to the question – why? Why did it have to happen this way? Why were we unable to prevent "IT"? Why were we not really able to steer the course of events towards a better end? How can it be that we have become "perpetrators" and feel like victims at the same time?

In this guide you have already learnt about many backgrounds and contexts that are completely unknown to even the most experienced counsellors, therapists and mediums.

Since we know from experience that all this knowledge alone is not sufficient to change our feelings, you can find two proven exercises below which will help you to clear up your feelings and relationships in a targeted way without having to contact certain people. Since the exercises include the universal divine level, it is also possible to clear up feelings towards people who are already dead.

Your personal freedom and autonomy is not dependent on the reactions of others but only on your individual willingness to universally clear up stressful events, relationships and emotions. After the exercises I will discuss this topic in more detail in section "Forgiveness for Parents and Other Perpetrators".

I call the following transformation texts "Please", "Ritual of Forgiveness to Clear up the Past and the Future" and "Absolute Forgiveness".

The poem and the first exercise help to get closer to the topic. They are a kind of motivating introduction to get you in the right frame of mind. The second exercise is a special gift, the personal effect of which can touch you deeply.

These texts also have the greatest impact if they are spoken aloud and from the heart.

5) Please

Just take this
little piece
of darkness
from my shoulders
to a place
where nobody
ever
has to burst
into tears
because of it –
please
take it away
I'll really stay
with you
to the end
of time.

Please
keep the hearts free
from the shadows
I have ever born
within human and other beings
in time and space.
Please
grant them holy freedom
for ever.
I am ready
to take on all
the shadows that belong to me.
Please
keep all beings free from them,
God.

6) Ritual of FORGIVENESS to Clear up the Past and the Future

I consciously merge with my divine being and as such I now become one with the divine source.

I ask for support and help with the clearing up process. I thank all the people who I have ever met on my journey of learning.

As the divine being that I AM, I now become one with the divine essence of all those people.

With each fibre of my Being, sincerely and from the bottom of my heart I ask all of you for forgiveness for all the sorrow and the pain that I might have caused you in one way or another.

Please forgive me.

I hereby sincerely beg you for forgiveness for any way that I have consciously or unconsciously hurt and humiliated you in your divinity. May the divine essence of healing and clarity pour into all those injuries now.

In the face of the divine source I hereby ask the Divine Father and the Divine Mother to give you the mercy of salvation and deliverance from all the dark shadows that my soul has cast upon you – in this or any other time.

I am now ready to take responsibility for all this. I could not act any other way on my path to learning. Please forgive me.

With all respect and in deep appreciation I wish you all happiness and prosperity on your onward journey. May everything that has happened before change for the best for all of you in a divine way, in joy and ease, in clarity and love.

For myself I also ask for the divine grace of release from all the dark shadows and issues that have mixed with my divine being because I took them on at some point in my journey. May these dark shadows lift now like fog that vanishes and be forever converted into unconditional love and divine freedom.

I am now ready to come to terms with all that has happened, in the power and purity of my divine essence. I am now ready to take on and fulfil my responsibility for my divine essence in dignity.

May we all be blessed as divine beings and be able to meet each other in a divine way, now and evermore.

30/03/2007

7) Absolute Forgiveness

I invite all people and souls to this space who are still connected to me in any way.

I ask the divine powers of heaven and earth to be here with us.

I ask these divine forces to flood all those spaces with divine healing light where my dark shadows have left their traces in your Being.

May all the burdensome energy connections that were created between us this way be dissolved for ever with divine help.

In the face of the divine I wholeheartedly ask all of you for forgiveness for anything I have done to hurt you, disappoint, humiliate, ignore or abuse you.

I am deeply saddened to feel all this today and to know the plight in which I have left you all alone.

I know that there were many times when I did not treat you with the dignity that we all deserve.

I am aware of your anger, your rage and even hatred.

I am sorry that we have shared all the dark fruits with each other – I do not think any of us have ever stilled our hunger with them.

I therefore beseech you all, here, today, to make peace with me and to brave a new beginning.

I beg you with all that I AM, with all the pain which I have also suffered, to forgive me all the sadness and coldness that bears my signature in your history.

None of it brought me happiness either and I would like to ask all of you to forgive me for everything I've done.

I am sorry that I have disappointed you so deeply, abandoned you and often left you alone. Today I am distraught at how I was ever able to stray so far away from myself. The divine being inside me is deeply shocked by all the grief that has been brought into your world by me and by how far we have distanced ourselves from each other because of that.

I think it is time to turn back and to nourish our souls with the power of good thoughts, in all mindfulness and with all the appreciation that we have developed on our way.

Before the darkness of the sad events throws new shadows between us I would like to remind you of the shining divinity which is the origin of all of us.

I for my part absolve you today from any guilt or responsibility with regards to myself and pray for all of us that we may receive the light of divine grace and that all the shadows in our karmic history may be dissolved.

I believe in love and the healing power of knowledge and understanding which is bound to have found a shining place in your heart also.

I am willing to do anything it takes to accept my part of the responsibility, just like today, here, in a divine way, and to transform it into a good power.

I thank each and every one of you who support me in being blessed with a loving heart.

I am looking forward to meeting you in a new divine freedom whenever you are ready for it.

I wholeheartedly wish each of you happiness and well-being on your onward journey to regain possession of your divine origin.

Thank you
16/01/2000

PS:
If you feel that all this lifts a burden off your shoulders; if saying these words of forgiveness takes dark shadows away from your soul and creates room for a new easiness; then and only then I also ask your forgiveness.

For only when we feel and understand this power will it truly be possible to brave a new beginning beyond time and space and embark on a new path where we honour our divinity in humility, love and dignity. To perhaps meet you again one day in this dignity will be my greatest joy.

Reader's service:

If you are working with the exercises and would like to print them on paper you will need two things.

1) The link to the PDF "Karmic Relationships Exercises" which I have prepared especially for that purpose.

Please go to the following website:
www.karmische-beziehung.de/links

– There you will find a link to the exercises in the section on chapter 7.

2) The password for access is: copyrightbesuca

As a further step to personal freedom and autonomy I would like to recommend that you should definitely check the origins and meaning of your own "spirituality" with the help of someone impartial, including with regard to possible trauma. Perhaps you could formulate your last question during the satsang as an intention and compare the information which you receive. What meaning do disciplines like reiki, diksha, yoga, etc. really have in your life? The answers could change your life. Even if there is a "healthy" form of "spirituality" for me, practice shows that many spiritual people are traumatised and developed their spirituality as a survival mechanism. As a reiki master, channel medium and reincarnation therapist I needed a long time to discover these connections. As a trauma therapist I therefore hope that your "spiritual journey" might lead you to our practice at some point. You won't have to hand in your tarot cards and spiritual stories at the entrance either. I promise.

Forgiveness for Parents and Other Perpetrators – Karmic Relationship between Victim and Perpetrator

It isn't really within your power to forgive parents or other people for mistreatment, abuse and mental cruelty that you have suffered at their hands. So do not worry if you do not completely succeed in this, even if this is something you would like to do because that's something that would agree with your life philosophy. That is not what this book is about! On the contrary. I would like to encourage you to finally put a halt to misunderstood experiments in forgiveness. Therapeutic practice shows that the risk is far too great at this point that you might make yourself a victim of your faith or your personal philosophy of life all over again. Do not force yourself into something that hurts you personally more than it helps, out of ideology and wishful thinking.

To turn the "other cheek" as well is one of the ideologies of perpetrator groups and religious packaging of forgiveness primarily serves the perpetrators.

If you try to forgive the perpetrators for misunderstood religious reasons you actually deepen the separation of your personality parts that were split off by their actions. Your "abused" childhood fragments simply feel betrayed by your forgiveness of the perpetrators and retreat even further. You thus primarily cement the existing web of lies and block the way to your own truth. After all, you are no longer allowed to be angry with a perpetrator whom you have already forgiven. I would like to invite your religious feelings here to primarily

374

protect the human being, namely yourself. Please do not turn yourself into a victim yet again. You will have time for forgiveness later, when you have completed your "healing process". Only then **can** it be an authentic feeling as well.

This may seem a bit over the top to you at this point but I would like to make the following quite clear: It is not your responsibility to forgive people who have become perpetrators against you! Any justification of a perpetrator's actions equals a betrayal of your own feelings and victim experience. Say goodbye to the idea of being able to give absolution to perpetrators. This is about the chance of finding ways of recognition and transformation on both sides which are completely independent of each other.

As long as you feel that you are in a position of power which gives you the ability to give "absolution" to someone else, you live in the position of a judge. This is a classic attitude of avoidance and misjudgement. Only the divine source can completely forgive seriously reformed people who committed a betrayal of humanity and unprotected life. In a "pseudo-power position" you live in a fixation on the perpetrator or perpetrators and are thus avoiding entering into real contact with the background to your own victim experience. Do not be seduced by the illusion that you are able to let other people squirm on your merciful "absolution hook". This would push you into the attitude of a perpetrator and you will not get any further. On the contrary. You bind yourself to this seductive power game and with that "hook" keep a permanent contact to the perpetrator. You will never get to the point this way where true forgiveness out of knowledge, compassion and your own "redemption" might actually become possible.

Therefore, if necessary, leave all the responsibility for what you have experienced with the respective persons and do it as impartially as possible. Stay true to yourself in your responsibility for your truth and your feelings. You would do better to forgive yourself first and foremost for defending the healing power of your healthy rage against the veiled guise of a "perfect world" that you have never experienced in reality. Make sure that you do not make yourself the victim of your faith or your personal worldview at this point. I hope this is clear enough.

Perpetrators should not demand absolution from their victims for the crimes that they have committed against them in the past because that way they lose the chance to carry the responsibility which has become apparent, in any kind of dignity.

For you as the perpetrator it is important to take full responsibility for all your actions. This is the first step in clearing up your personal history – from which your role of perpetrator could arise.
If you take this path you will eventually get to the point where you really understand and feel what you have done and how it could have happened. When you then say "I am sorry" and "I beg your forgiveness for everything" from the bottom of your heart, it will find resonance in the divine source that you will feel as the light of divine grace. You should follow this path in humility and dignity until the dark shadows of your his-

tory are purified with the light of divine grace. You do not have to contact your victims directly and continue to burden them in order to achieve this. If a victim seeks contact with you, take this chance in all your honesty and compassion. Seek ways to make up for your deeds without putting the dignity of the victim in question. Stay in your dignity as well and do not let yourself be blackmailed. This is about the recognition of responsibility and about human dignity on both sides. This should happen with the greatest mutual respect and mindfulness.

As a perpetrator you still bear the burden of the entanglement with very dark, suppressed events and emotions of a family history that overwhelms you in an uncontrollable manner again and again. With the knowledge you gain from this guide you can begin to change this. Search for additional help from people who will accompany you with respect for your dignity.

For you as a victim it is important not to let yourself be overburdened by the perpetrator all over again.

With the help of the exercises you can deal with the issue of forgiveness in your own way, at your own speed and may possibly even include perpetrators in your life in this forgiveness work, if that is suitable for you. For you it is important to most of all stay true to yourself as an advocate for your injuries. You are entitled to a healthy dose of anger at all attempts by others to belittle the traumas you have suffered. Do not however get stuck in this anger and do not stay there. Open yourself to a healthy and useful way to work through your personal "victim history".

If you take this path, you will eventually get to the point where you really understand and feel what you have suffered - in your childhood perhaps. With this painful truth you will gradually regain a sense of a new "wholeness" which contains the strength to find a new zest for life. This new attitude to life will perhaps one day give you a strange urge to make peace with the perpetrators in your life in a new way. Then your "I now absolve you from all guilt and responsibility for my person", spoken from the heart, will ignite a light of special grace in your heart and the heart of the "perpetrator". Then, in even deeper insight than ever before, you will feel the importance and power of true forgiveness.

Particularly the entanglement through KARMA in karmic relationships will become more conscious to you in higher complexity. The quality of an offense can change in a positive way and contribute to the maturation of your personality if you accept the challenge to explore the deeper background of your karmic relationship with the "perpetrator". This includes understanding the dynamics and "self-sabotage" by perpetrator-loyal parts inside you. Examine all your relationships this way that are still marked by victim-perpetrator dynamics and change them step by step.

Search for professional help to dissolve and convert symbiotic entanglements with perpetrators in your life. This is teamwork, similar to the removal of a tumour. The individual steps lead to the expansion of your consciousness and change your inner psychological structures.

As a positive side effect you will attract a partner on the love relationship level who does not have to encounter you as a perpetrator anymore but lives the love in your heart together with you in a new dimension. This love will be supported by a new freedom, independence and autonomy which perhaps may seem completely unrealistic to you right now.

Blaming, the ability to love and dream partners
As long as there are still "perpetrators" in your life with whom you associate highly stressful feelings that you have not yet converted into knowledge and power, a part of you is still living in a victim role. In an unresolved karmic relationship, this part usually lives in a reproachful attitude and waits for a "making up for the offence" to which you have bound yourself for an unspecified period of time. You may even be projecting this "blaming" attitude on "all men" or "all women" – even if only unconsciously. You should simply be aware of this so that you can separate these energies from your dream partnership. That's because your dream partner will definitely register your unresolved anger and the seething hatred inside you with the sensitivity of their "radar" and will probably refrain from getting too close to you if they cannot be sure that it is not directed at them as well. Therefore, always give the most room in your heart to your capacity to love.

My recommendation:
Wear your justified anger and your hatred – whenever it bubbles up – like a vest which you can also take off. Do not use such emotions as a body lotion though if you want to meet a partner who is able to give you tender loving care and make you feel good.

I recommend you find out for yourself and check what really serves your own recovery and wholeness. You can check this, for example, by employing the constellation of an intention. That is the easiest way to make sure that you avoid persuading yourself of something that does not correspond to reality.

Any kind of forgiveness work which has as its goal to forgive the perpetrator always carries the danger of denying and playing down the offence that was committed as well as one's own victim experience. If you forgive the partner who hit you, it will be easier for you to stay with them or go back to them again. This process cements your victim attitude and shows that something is working inside you that makes you put yourself at the perpetrator's disposition as a victim. Here you would misuse the forgiveness process in order not to put your victim role in question. At the same time you become a perpetrator against yourself.

The forgiveness process is meaningful in a context where we come into contact with and recognise our own perpetrator status or victim experience. Contact with perpetrators is usually counterproductive for the respective victims, as each contact with the perpetrator leads to a new trauma.
The recognition of perpetrator status and victim experience leads from an illusionary longing for an ideal world to the truth and reality of one's own life history.

Perhaps an image might help:
Does it really make sense to stay in the lion's cage or to return to it again and again to forgive the lion for biting your arm off?

Do you really feel good caring for your father / mother who has humiliated or abused you as a child, sexually, physically or psychologically?

From my experience, such caring actions and situations where victims care for their perpetrators are always accompanied by illusory wishful thinking and acting. This happens because of childhood soul fragments which desperately cling to the hope that one day they might hear a good word or receive praise or possibly even a small token of love from mom or dad. This illusion does not end with the death of the parents.

If you're thinking along the lines of revenge and retribution, please do not make the mistake or error to seek revenge on partners or innocent children of perpetrators in order to cause harm to the perpetrator. It may be that this person will not even notice it. Perpetrators are split personalities who are not in touch with their feelings. Other people play only very minor roles and if necessary they are replaced according to their optimal purpose. With such vengeful action you would open your very own perpetrator cycle in which you are the only perpetrator. Is that what you want?

Revenge entangles you in endless spirals. Revenge as well as forgiveness rituals are survival mechanisms that distract from clearing up one's own victim role. Vigilante justice will not dissolve one's own trauma but instead add new ones. You will not achieve any sustainable change in the perpetrators that way. I hope you will not need any time behind bars to think about that. Your life is too precious to be lost in the undertow of perpetrator structures. You would do better to use all your courage to clear up the causes for such dynamics in your life.

If necessary, get appropriate help to get out such situations.

Point of Reference:

**Forgiveness or revenge do not dissolve or clear up any trauma.
They rather hinder the recognition and processing of relationships with people who have traumatised you.**

Forgiveness is usually marked by illusionary wishful thinking and is often used as a survival strategy which down-plays the seriousness of the events.

In my experience, true forgiveness beyond religion and spirituality is only possible after you have worked through your own victimhood and mental split. It is not necessary for the healing process of a traumatised person to forgive the perpetrators. However, feelings of anger, hatred or revenge create emotional bonds between you and perpetrators as well as perpetrator-victim structures!

Point of Reference:
Misguided attempts at forgiveness lead away from one's own feelings and split personality parts before "healing" can be achieved!
Even if this turns your worldview upside down: Victims are not responsible for the forgiveness, absolution or care of perpetrators. Neither within the family nor in partnerships.

Please make sure that you do not become a perpetrator yourself due to a misunderstood sense of responsibility. If you are still bound to perpetrators by contracts, powers of attorney or similar things, organise and delegate, if necessary, the supply or care for this person(s) and keep as much distance as possible. This recommendation explicitly includes any individuals who have become perpetrators directly (violence, abuse, humiliation,...) or indirectly (silence, failure to provide assistance,...).

Conclusion – The Reckoning – Help – Hotline – Partnership

In order to survive trauma and to be able to protect oneself from further trauma, the vigilance and the perception of one's own senses expands further and further, to "infinity". This "radar", developed as an alarm- and early warning system, promotes "supernatural" – "clairvoyant" skills which are often seen as "spiritual" gifts. The truth is however that the skills of many mediums originate in an early childhood trauma. Since they are so far away from themselves, they can feel everything from everyone else; they have the images, dreams and feelings of others and almost no connection to themselves.

Such mediums live in their own trauma blindness and therefore do not see the relevant connections when it comes to their clients. Their own difficulties in relationships are often hidden or taken as unavoidable – without putting into question their own "calling" to advise other people in these matters.

This very often leads to vague misleading answers which cannot uncover the true backgrounds to life blockages. For years I did not understand this, but whenever I consulted mediums, clairvoyants, fortune tellers or other people regarding these questions, I observed this phenomenon and from today's perspective got nothing but disappointing results. I have tested a number of consultants – also on recommendation – over the last 25 years and always got basically the same result:

No one could explain to me clearly what was really going on with me. "Everything (private, business, financial) should actually be working just fine in your case...," was the classic wall which I felt myself nailed to. But beyond that I could not move an inch. Not even one little hint that something must have been wrong or must have happened in my childhood. If you have also heard this "actually" often already then you know now: This is a massive indication of TRAUMA.

Pain, the cause of which nobody can find, is also part of this. You would therefore do better to invest your money in trauma and identity constellations than in hotlines provided by ignorant advisors. If you yourself are working in this field as a medium I recommend that you delve into with the issue of TRAUMA immediately (see "Karmic Relationships and TRAUMA") and dissolve your own trauma blindness. Then you will be able to help many people in the future to discover this phenomenon and to approach the process of dealing with it in a sensible way. This way, new opportunities will be freed up to understand difficult situations in a partnership and with your help perhaps to deal with them without the need for a separation.

With this in mind I hope that my documentary about karmic relationships managed to lift a few veils for you and gave you new courage to roll up your sleeves and work on your personal life and love happiness. It is worth it!

Always Keep in Mind:

As long as a person / soul is still caught up in
TRAUMA, they cannot fully ascend to their divinity.
Every single separation of parts of one's personality
will be reflected in an unhappy, incomplete love
relationship. With this in mind, your partner is never
the problem but always just a status report of the
mirror of your own soul. So do not waste any time
trying to reshape your partner and to mould them
to your needs.
**Otherwise you are definitely working
at the wrong construction site!**

If any questions still remain unanswered, I look forward to
receiving your request for a personal consultation or participation in a seminar.

For everything else, I would like to encourage you to apply a
very effective and proven method. With this motto I started
my own journey many years ago. Therefore I think that this
guide cannot find a more dignified ending.

What Could You Learn for Your Relationships from This Part?

From Part 7, I would like you to take away at least this one thing:

**If nobody can help you
to deal with your problem
become someone
who can help others
with the same issue.**

15/05/1999

PS:

If you saw the light on one issue or another when you read this book, I would be delighted if you could radiate it out into the world in your own way. Who knows? Perhaps it will at some point light up even my way in the dark night.

Check-Out

I hope you had an insightful journey through your relationship life and are feeling solid ground under your feet again. Do you remember the luggage check before the start of this adventure? How many animals do you still have in your luggage? Do you still have "ten spiders, one rat and one skunk" as a companion? Perhaps you could simply write me a brief report on your experience.

Perhaps in your further life you will ask yourself the following question again and again: What should I do now? For such situations I would like to give you a universal four step rule to take with you on your way. This formula will help you to answer any life question more easily.

<u>Four Step Rule to Clear Up Life Questions</u>

Recognition – the red light – be aware of the situation

Understanding – the meaning – cause, backgrounds, why am I experiencing this?

Solution – take your foot off the gas pedal – the first reaction, immediate measures, what needs to be done?

Decision – where do you really want to go? – answer life, correct your course

You can easily measure the extent of your personal freedom if you look at the room for manoeuvre you have in situations and areas of life which are important to you. For the analysis and optimisation of your room for manoeuvre, a few bullet points on the four universal steps may help you.

Recognition

- Where do I stand?

- What is on my mind?

- What overburdens me?

- What do I not understand?

- What would I like to change?

Guiding principles:

The will to change is the first door to insight.

Everything that is in your consciousness can also be consciously changed.

Understanding

- Why has my life turned out like this rather than any other way?

- Which experience of the past still determines my actions today?

- Which part of my life have I forgotten or not understood and why?

- Which feelings are really mine and which external feelings are influential now?

- What did I do before? Which impulse brought me into this situation?

Guiding principles:

As long as I live in foreign feelings and am entangled with the histories of others, I cannot and do not have to perceive my own feelings and my own history.

When I process the trauma I can gradually start to live my dream.

Solution

- What should and can I definitely do immediately?

- How can I expand my room for manoeuvre?

- Which foreign feelings or foreign influences would I like to separate myself from?

- What pattern of behaviour can I recognise in myself right now? Would I like to change it?

- Have I slipped into a victim or perpetrator attitude that I can get out of again?

Guiding principles:

The freedom to change my life grows with my willingness and ability to recognise structures that have previously determined my life.

Dependence and heteronomy are, among other things, the consequence of illusions, ignorance, suppression of truth and unwillingness to take responsibility.

Decision

- How would the person decide that you would like to be?

- How would your role model decide?

- How would you decide if you were guaranteed not to fail?

- Act yourself or have others do things to/for you?

- "Wish-come-true at the push a button" therapy or lifelong deep personal development?

- Which response or decision will lead me to at least one of my top three important goals for the year or for my life?

Guiding principles:

In my life, in my sense, a change is possible if I take complete responsibility for it.

The clearer my life goals are, the easier it is for me to make clear, targeted decisions.

What I have thought about relationships, marriage, love and sexuality until now is not necessarily true. I now decide on a way of thinking and acting that supports me in living happy relationships.

Those who understand
what separates them,
do not have to separate themselves
from what they do not understand.

Angels Do Not Cry

You did not see me,
when you
stepped into the free space
and so I noticed
the expression
on your face
which I only
know from people
who lay their fate
into foreign hands
and are at peace
with that.

For a moment
I forgot about
the meaning of the church
in the background
and let myself be touched
by your fate
which I had never touched
from this perspective
before.

Suddenly you saw me
and looked at me
as if at a ghost

but it seemed not to be uncommon to you
to see it.
So you had not forgotten about me
to this day,
in all these years –
deep inside me
something started to understand.

You thus passed
by the ghost
in your world
and inside me
a dam of tears broke
out of me
quite suddenly.

As I was sobbing,
something gently touched
my hand before my eyes –
I fell into your arms
like a child.

Very quietly
I heard you say:
Angels do not cry.

15/12/2007

Further Information

Books by Franz Ruppert
Splits in the Soul – ISBN: 978-0955968327
Symbiosis and Autonomy, 2010 – ISBN 978-0-9559683-3-4

Essence and the latest science! ***
Trauma, Fear and Love | ISBN 978-0955968365
Early Trauma | ISBN 978-0955968372
My Body My Trauma My I | ISBN 978-0955968389

Vivian Broughton
Becoming Your True Self

Bessel van der Kolk
The Body Keeps the Score

Novels by affected people / experiences

… helpful in order to for example use "trigger points" to jog specific memories of similar feelings you had yourself; Take care to read these in small doses and be mindful of your feelings!

These books are anything but "Fast Food":
Truddi Chase, Scream | DE ISBN: 978-3404614981
Ulla Fröhling, Our Father in Hell | DE ISBN: 978-3404616251
Terry M. Balthasar, *Protected by the Herd*
DE ISBN: 978-3940868503

Audio Book Recommendation

Arno Gruen, *Betrayed Love – False Gods,*
DE ISBN: 978-3942402026
T. Harv Eker, *Secrets of the Millionaire Mind*

FILM RECOMMENDATIONS

I am the Other Woman, with Katja Riemann among others, directed by: Margarethe von Trotta

Shutter Island, with Leonardo DiCaprio among others, directed by: Martin Scorsese

Internet Contacts

Franz Ruppert www.franz-ruppert.de - International

Trauma constellations in seminars or single sessions according to Prof Dr Franz Ruppert:

Germany
Aurora Wolf & Bernd Casel
www.koerper-trauma-ich.de
D-73773 Aichwald – Praxis & Studio Aichwald

Nutrition International **www.vitamin-leben.com**

      direct-link Q10 www.Q10.vitamin-leben.de
      direct-link AOP www.AOP.vitamin-leben.de

On the topics of reconciliation, help and donations:
http://www.amma.de

For me, Amma's charitable work is beyond any doubt. It leaves room for any size and form of your desired engagement. Trust your feeling. What flows here is blessed in a special way and love.

Key

Those who
do not know
what
still separates them
from love, luck
and ease,
remain
split
where they are –
if they do not search for
ways to disentangle.

How to Contact the Author

Bernd Casel
Schanbacher Straße 2/1
D-73773 Aichwald

Email: besuca@besuca.com
Please submit any questions in German
or arrange a translator.

Practice and Studio Aichwald
Practice for integrative therapeutic procedures
Internet: www.koerper-trauma-ich.de
Email: kontakt@koerper-trauma-ich.de

**Every human being
has their own fate
and if we manage
to deal with it
in dignity, appreciation
and love,
then one day
something big will grow from it.**

Legal Notice

no legal responsibility and no liability for any damage resulting from the use or non-use of this guide or parts thereof.

Furthermore, the author assumes no responsibility for the accuracy, completeness and timeliness of the information presented. Any liability is therefore excluded.

Links
This guide contains links to external websites of third parties, the content of which the author has no influence over. Therefore, the author assumes no responsibility for the content of these third party contents. The respective providers or operators of these linked pages are always responsible for their contents. The linked pages were checked for possible legal violations at the time of linking. No illegal content was detected at the time of linking. However, a permanent control of the linked pages is not reasonable without concrete evidence of a legal violation. Upon notification of any such violations, the respective links will be removed from this book immediately.

Data Protection Declaration:
Privacy
The use of my websites is usually possible without providing personal information. Insofar as personal data (e. g. name, address or e-mail address) is collected on pages, this is always done on a voluntary basis, as far as possible. This data will not be passed on to third parties without your explicit consent.

Data transmission over the Internet (e. g. while communicating by e-mail) may contain security vulnerabilities. A complete protection of data against unauthorised access by third parties is not possible.

The use of the contacts published due to the imprint obligation by third parties for transmission of unsolicited advertising and information materials is hereby expressly prohibited. The operators of the websites reserve the right to take legal action in case of unsolicited advertising information such as spam e-mails.

Participation in affiliate programs

Bernd Casel is a participant in the affiliate program of PM International and Amazon Europe S.à.r.l. and partner of the advertising programme designed to provide a medium for sites with which advertising fees can be earned through the placement of advertising and links on amazon.de.

Invitation

What if all people worldwide gave each other a helping hand and supported each other in order to break free from past entanglements?

What if 1,000, 10,000, 100,000 people in each country dared to make a new start?

What if you actively participated in this new beginning?

The earnings gained from this guide will finance the translation into other languages that follow this vision. I am therefore full of deep appreciation for each of your recommendations and any other assistance.

If the spirit of this book managed to touch you and you would like to write a review of this guide, I would like to thank you in advance, also on behalf of the people who, just like you, feel the impulse to use this information for their own benefit. Who knows, maybe this way, new inspiring relationships will develop that suddenly enrich your life, too.

I am delighted about any honest reader's opinion and thank you wholeheartedly for your interest and openness towards this book.

I express my thanks to you
from the bottom of my heart
for each positive impulse from this book
which you integrate into your life and
your relationships.

Epilogue

According to a survey among about 34 million global citizens and members of the Avaaz Community at the beginning of 2014, almost 39% of the participants referred to themselves as spiritual but not religious. I do not know how you feel about this and what description might fit your way of life in the most accurate way. I was one of those who were asked to participate in the survey and looking back, the description of "spiritual but not religious" already applied to me when I was about 15 years old. I remember the time before that only fragmentarily; I have not been "religious" ever since I gained the ability to think for myself. At around the time of my fifteenth year of age I read a lot and was particularly intrigued by a book on parapsychology which I had bought with my pocket money. At that time, I tried to explore the relationship between me and the world especially through reading, yoga and meditation, until I was about 20. Even today, the topic of psychology and relationships still has not lost its fascination for me. On the contrary. Again and again, important insights into these issues have saved my life and have become part of my profession.

An insight I gained less than ten years ago is of such deep significance as was the feeling of freedom that enveloped me in my childhood when I was finally able to read and write. It is to do with my personal style of spirituality. To a large extent it turned out to be a survival mechanism from my early childhood. My spirituality was therefore a "consequence of something" rather than the ultimate cause with which I believed to be able to gain access to the world as it

was when I was a teenager. In such survival mechanisms, the uncomfortable truth which I do not conceal
from you in this guide means suppressing, forgetting
and denying the world as it really is and the way you
have experienced it. That is what this guide is also
about. This "forgetting" might not be such a bad thing
in itself, if "this man" or "that woman" lives alone on an
island. In interpersonal relationships, circumstances
where we cannot recognise causes and effects for
what they are or even confuse them, regularly lead to
greater irritation as well as private and business conflicts. Since we are consciously or unconsciously
excluding a part of the world as it really was or is, or
even turning it upside down, we get into ever greater
difficulties as we age. We cannot and do not always
want to admit this.

Sometimes there is also a lack of appropriate help. I
spent almost 30 years of my life searching for it. In order to unlock the secrets of my life and my "karmic"
relationships, I had to stake everything on one card
again and again. Without a safety net. Without a life or
money back guarantee. There was practically no room
for holidays, leisure and entertainment. I wanted to
know the whole truth and this was only possible without escape hatches.

Truths are not always easy. Especially difficult to understand are those phases of life and their
consequences where we can only survive by closing
ourselves completely to the truth. Some experiences
are associated with such deep injuries and fears that
we have to give up our mental unity in order to survive.
The part of our personality that we had to split off is

what we then unconsciously search for in our relationships and are surprised by its incompleteness. Perhaps you have met people who have blocked out so much from their world that they do not recognise their own difficulties. Recognition means to accept the truth as it is. The willingness for this can be practiced.

Perhaps it is also time to accept that biological parenthood does not automatically mean that parents have entered into the honourable task of becoming father and mother. If I consider the topic pregnancy dispassionately, it is, in my experience, often an unwanted "by-product" and even to people who want to have children often happens in a moment that's "perceived" as inopportune. More important than the question of circumstances is the question of what quality of bond, emotion and love the parents expect their child with and accompany it with after birth. Being a planned child of highly traumatised parents is traumatic for a child from the start. The joy of anticipation on the part of the male parent is traumatic for the child even while still in the womb, if this man has sadistic tendencies or is a paedophile.

Even a "real" planned child who arrives at the "wrong time" sets off a chain of questions and challenges for the parents. Apprenticeships, training, studies, the relationship and the pregnancy itself are put into question. If the decision for the child is positive, the unclarified questions result, depending on social environment and current life situation, in an area of tension that accompanies and burdens the parent-child relationship from the beginning. Love easily gets lost here.

From a child's perspective, a woman who gives birth to a child but does not take any responsibility for the protection of the child's dignity and integrity, never even began to be a mother.

From a child's perspective, a man who has fathered a child but does not take any responsibility for the protection of the child's dignity and integrity, never even began to be a father.

It is therefore no wonder that so many children and adults live in the illusion that in reality they have a different father or mother.

Healthy relationships during childhood are a prerequisite for the child's development of a healthy psyche. Adults who find themselves in unhealthy, unhappy relationships have, as a rule, grown up with people in their environment with whom the development of healthy relationships was difficult or even impossible. In such a climate, a child's own soul parts are often split off in order to protect themselves from the external violence, manipulation, lack of love or liveliness. As adults we often have difficulties in coming into contact with the truth of our own childhood and our own split-off parts. Here, therapeutic support is ideal.

In this expanded book edition I have developed a few thoughts for you which touch on various themes. Use the guiding principles that affect you while reading the book in order to approach a topic in your own way. Try to keep reading these sentences for a few days and simply let their effect on you develop. A good time is in the morning before the start of your daily activities and in the evening before going to sleep. You can support their effectiveness by saying those phrases out loud while reading.

8) Guiding Principles on Contemplation

Every child has the right, not the obligation, to love its parents, no matter what they have done to it.

Even before birth every child already has the right to personal liberty and integrity of mind and body.

Any child whose right to integrity is disregarded by others must split.

Any adult who puts the love and relationship to his/her own parents, siblings or other persons above his/her right to his/her own integrity and freedom becomes a perpetrator against himself/herself and has to split again and again.

Any child who has been traumatised by the parents survives by fleeing into the imagination of an illusionary, rescuing, healing love that lets everything be good again.

As sad as only a child can be, is what the adult becomes later who was never really allowed to be a child, for as long as he still lives in the splits of his childhood.

Any adult can regain their own freedom and autonomy.

Parents who did not have the dignity to protect their child's right to personal freedom and integrity have never begun to be father or mother to the child.

9) Guiding Principles on Contemplation II

These buildings blocks touch on specific traumas and their consequences. They are still in the development phase. I would like to offer them to you as motivation at this point.

As a child who knows the truth inside me I may now recognise that the adult who has grown up from this child can now ensure our safety by his success.

A part of us has now grown up and this part is me.

Now I have become an adult myself whose success in harming me I had to prevent as a child.

As the adult I am today I can protect the child inside me from harm by being successful myself.

As the adult I am today, I can recognise that as a child I had to prevent the success of adults in harming me in order to survive.

As the adult I am today, I can recognise that as a child I had to prevent the success of adults in killing me in order to survive. With my own success I can now protect myself more easily from adults who want to harm me.

As the child who knows the truth inside me I may now recognise that the adult who has grown up from this child can provide for our freedom with his financial success.

Again and again we are confronted by questions concerning methods and techniques that are useful in terms of treatment or self-help. I therefore want to add a small supplement to Part 6 here – "Counselling under the Microscope".

Control and Survival Techniques for Stress, Trauma, Obesity etc.

Surely you also know "tense situations" and can imagine situations or events where tension reaches intolerable levels. If our protection programmes to relieve stress are running at full capacity and cannot stop an overwhelming, threatening situation, we have to suppress and split off the event we experienced. With that event, the physical strain is also "frozen". The longer such tension stays in the body, the greater the perceived pressure often becomes. This can lead to various symptoms and pains. Headaches, migraines, high blood pressure, a stiff neck and the like are known consequences. An approach in terms of self-help is to "unload" the pressure and tension in the body in order to change the pain level and the symptoms. Various methods provide relief here. The relaxation which may be achieved here should not be confused with the resolution of trauma though. Such methods attempt to keep the consequences of something within a manageable range. Obesity is also something that shows itself as a "consequence of something" on a physical level. Regular attempts at weight loss by fasting or mental techniques do not clear up or dissolve the cause of obesity.

Whether you discharge pent-up anger, stress or trauma with sports, relaxation techniques or "shaking off", the cause will not be cleared up this way. Even if you experience temporary relaxation as an effect of your actions.

Once you have developed an awareness of trauma, once you have worked through the events that have traumatised you, once the events and the perpetrators have been named and recognised by you as such, the phase begins in which the resolution of psychological splits by trauma becomes possible. This is the way you can gradually regain your mental unity. Survival structures and consequences of trauma such as anorexia, obesity, anger, stress, headaches etc. can only change when the underlying trauma is fully processed.

By definition, physical discharge and relaxation techniques do not differentiate between traumas. They usually only have the "discharge" as their inevitably recurring focus. This may well be helpful as an additional measure to ongoing trauma therapy. Any technique that helps to reduce the intake of drugs is definitely beneficial for the body. Be critical if such a method is offered to you on its own and as trauma therapy. In case of symbiosis traumas you are in danger otherwise of spending your life processing foreign traumas instead of separating yourself from them. If I have a hole in the roof, I can of course spend years carrying away the accumulated water in buckets without ever addressing the real cause.

Therefore my final advice is:
No matter who you work with and which method you use to process your personal life issues: make sure that they do not sell you the "bucket" alone.

Those who only "address" the consequences
never have to care about the causes!

I would be glad if the impulses and information in this guide inspired and encouraged you to conduct your relationship with yourself and others with greater freedom and autonomy.

What if enlightenment is only the last vanishing point that consciousness is able to create whilst excluding its own Self?

Sandspring

From the springs of life
the thirsty
is oft unable
to drink
because his head
is buried
too deep
in the sand
or in his work.

Revenge

I know
that you don't really
have a chance
against that force inside you,
that burns like a fire
and cries out for vengeance.

I know
that nobody
can ever stop
this force,
other than
the part of you
that recognises
this force.

Blessed Moments

Sometimes
the hand remembers
in the middle
of the movement
that it can stop in its tracks -
cherish these roots
of blessed moments
of spiritual freedom
in yourself
and in others.

Sometimes
a word remembers
as it's passing someone's lips
that there might be a nicer sound -
cherish the beginnings
of such humanity
in yourself
and in others,
wherever you encounter them.

Stay

I initially thought
that it was only about
disarming
a time bomb -

I did not know
that it
lies in a mine field
that separates me
from you.

Evening Breeze

Softly as a dream

that quietly only

enters my soul,

your gaze fell

into my eyes

with a charming radiance

which seemed to originate

from a fountain of life

deep inside you.

With this tender greeting

you touched me more deeply

than even closest proximity

could ever do before.

I just stood still

in this timeless embrace

and simply watched

where the train disappeared to

with you.

The cool evening breeze

was what finally

reminded me

of all the things

we so casually

call life.

Never before

and never since

have I touched it in quite this way

.

Don't ever stop
being yourself,
start to be yourself
again and again
and always allow yourself
to change.

Тайна кармических отношений | RU

978-3-7469-6129-3 (Paperback)

978-3-7469-6130-9 (Hardcover)

978-3-7469-6131-6 (e-Book)

www.platz.besuca.com

Space for hard drives and small devices

iMac* accessories
Hard disk holder for 24 and 27 inches

* iMAC is a registered trademark of
Apple Inc. in the USA

Printed in Great Britain
by Amazon